Adriano Maccone - Alessandro Martinelli **The City at the End of the Underground**

Adriano Maccone. An amateur photographer, he has traveled to several countries for his photographic projects, that concern the contemporary world and life. Among his recent photographic books, "Tag: pride and prejudice" and "Made in Taiwan." (adrianomaccone.eu)

Alessandro Martinelli. Involved in research and didactical activities about the contemporary urban condition at the Accademia di architettura in Mendrisio, at the Berlage institute, at the Barcelona institute of Architecture, at the i2a Vico Morcote, at the Canadian Centre for Architecture, at the Archivio Cattaneo, today he is assistant professor in Landscape architecture at the Chinese Culture University in Taipei, and works together with BIAS Architects on architectural and curatorial projects that address the contemporary public space.

This book, by Adriano Maccone and Alessandro Martinelli, concerns the image of the city at the terminal stations of various underground mass-transit systems in Europe and the Far East. With the objective to document and understand what constitutes the margin of the urban phenomenon in an age of globalization and urbanization, the book collects and complements a selection of materials from a photographic project that has been developed by Adriano Maccone over a number of years. Offering the possibility for comparative perspectives and some theoretical insights at the intersection of photography and the city, the book finally hopes to contribute from a global perspective to the awareness of the complex relations between the city, urban space, and urban design.

this book must be quoted
Maccone, Adriano, & Martinelli, Alessandro (2018).
The City at the End of the Underground.
Trento: Listlab.

index

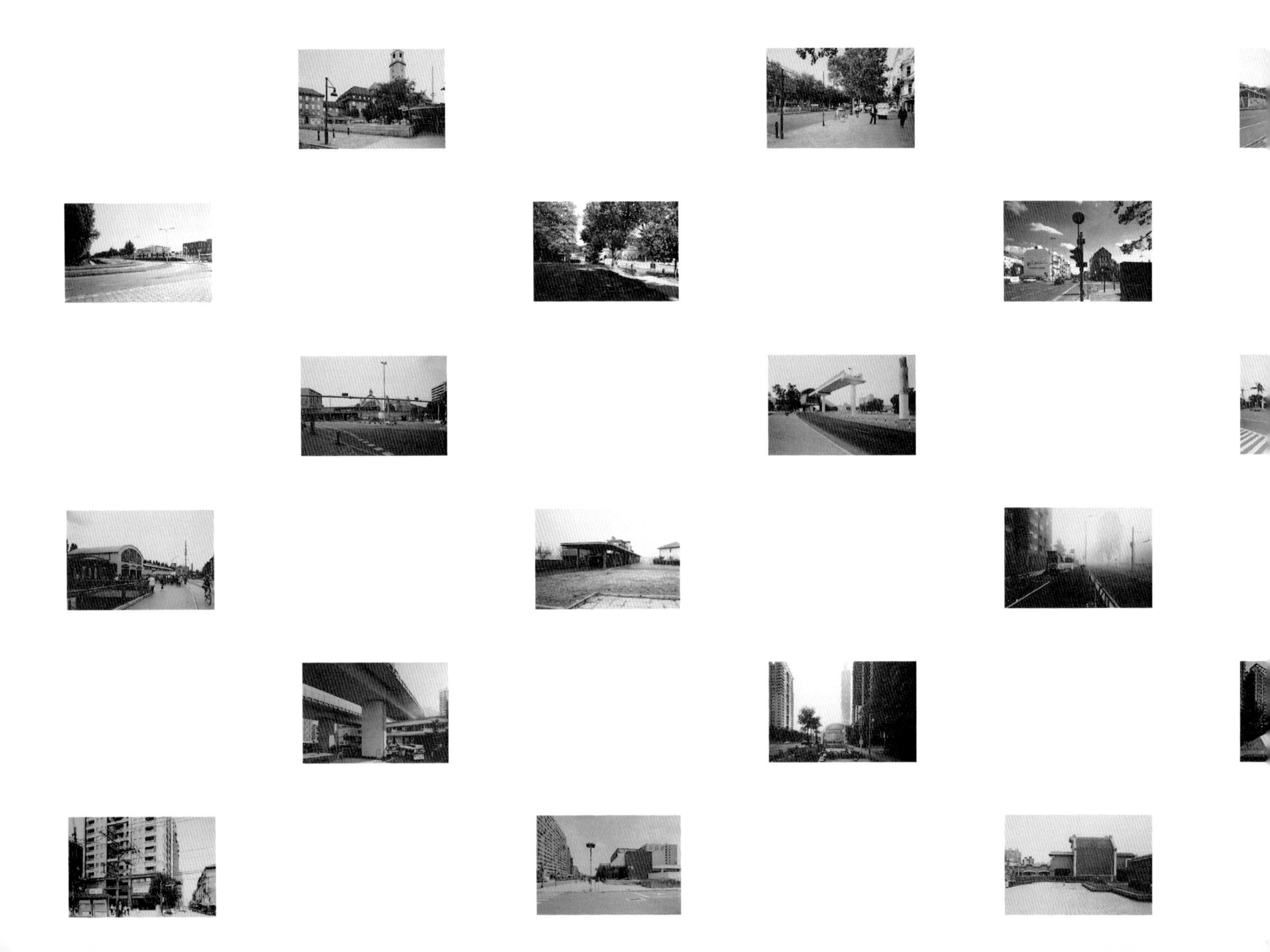

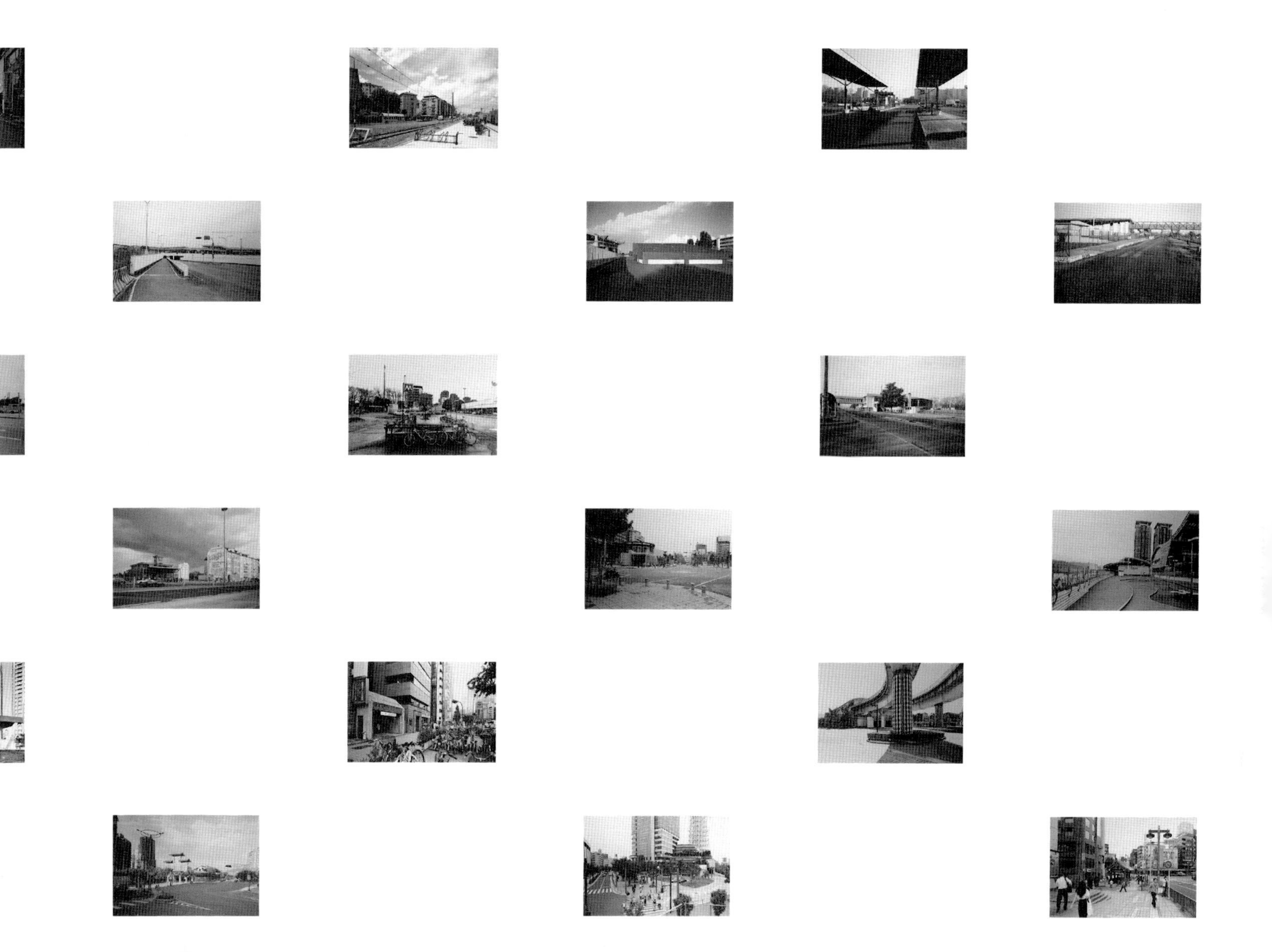

The City at the End of the Underground

Sightings of the urban condition

by Adriano Maccone

To some extent, “The City at the End of the Underground” is a photographic project that records a personal experience. The subject is the public space at the terminal stations of the subway system in a series of cities around the world. The work was carried out during 2015 and 2017 but participates a much longer research that I have been working on for a few years on.

My original goal was to develop some images where the background is occupied by a metropolitan setting and a subway station is in the foreground. Then, this simple idea went on to be repeated in diverse places. Finally, the pictures were taken in few cities that greatly differ in terms of history, culture, climate, but are associated because of those urban issues that most of the cities and people around the world today share, i.e. overcrowding, traffic, etc... Indeed, half of world population now lives in urban areas with these kinds of problems. Nowadays the biggest cities can host tens of millions of people. They have become the biggest and most complex structures ever built by mankind. Overtime they evolved into borderless and almost infinite concrete jungles. In fact almost 60% of the European population lives in them and utilises some sort of public transport to commute from the suburbs to the city centres. Housing markets follow the trend, too. In the light of this, transport systems have become the heart of contemporary societies and economies. Not by chance, the European Council of Spatial Planners is promoting a vision of European development characterized by a network of cities where diffused accessibility is provided to all who live, work, and visit there.[1]
If the very first example of underground mass transit dates back to the late 19th century -i.e. the London Tube- and only few capitals set up a system before the 50s of the last century. Since the 70s a number of projects were initiated in order to cope with rising car traffic and related environmental problems. However subway systems are not only built as an attempt to solve these problems. Their architecture is built in such a way that aesthetic concepts inevitably have to connect with

the surroundings. So, they are the combination of needs and culture, engineering systems and design styles, economics and social sciences.

This is the first aspect of the photographic subject at stake in this book. In order to portray this, I have been working with a Linhof view camera with roll film holders 6x9 and a Schneider Lens 58 mm. The reasons of this unified choice -as well as the black and white film- are to be found in the attempt to keep stylistic unity across the work. As far as practicable, I have used angles, shots, and perspectives so as that those shapes of buildings and urban spaces could play a significant role within the composition of the photographic image.

I took the subway to reach all the places that I shot. This way, I arrived on site without the distractions and stress deriving from car driving. The sequence of light and shadow, movement and waiting, that is given by the subway provided me with some expectations of those shapes, volumes, areas of my urban subject well before I could reach the destination and portray it on the 120 mm film. Then, as I have already written in the premises of my previous books "Tag: Price and Prejudice" and "Made in Taiwan," my images were just "written in light." Indeed, the verb "to photograph" derives from the ancient Greek words φωτός (photos), genitive of φῶς (phos) as "light," and γραφή (graphé) as "drawing." Considering that the subject of the pictures is given well before the photographic action, I can only push the button and capture the light in the right moment. This allows light to be memorized on a chemical media (the film for the analogical camera) or an electronic one (the sensor of the digital camera). So, I can only be the "reader of the light" that takes place in front of me. Due to this, my images simply frame the visual experience of the built environment at the end of the subway, where the actuality of the urban condition starts being questioned.

I started this project by portraying the fourteen terminals of Taipei city subway and the four of Kaohsiung, then followed by some in Dubai, Amsterdam, Milano, Berlin, and Tokyo. At a certain moment, the Asian cities started to play against the European ones. This way, the work has become sort of a personal quest about the effects of planning, urban design, and architecture in two very different geographical and cultural areas. I have wondered about the actuality of the political declarations behind the respective planning and design, with respect of the local cultural identities, the histories, and the socio-economic contexts. I have wondered about the possibility of some visible difference within the outcomes of the design approach and culture in the West and East.

As we all know, academic researchers use comparative methodologies for various purposes. For example, comparative anatomy is the study of similarities and differences within the body of the species as evidence for an interpretation of evolution. Comparative linguistics is concerned with the reconstruction of language roots and the pathways of linguistic differentiation. Comparative law is the study of legal systems in diverse countries, so as to investigate legitimacy and question their adequacy. The comparative studies define the planning and landscape disciplines, too. This is because they can offer a critical perspective over the quality of the environment, land protection, the conservation of landscape, that are those great challenges of today in the light of the urbanization of our world. Here, photography can provide a structural contribution, and the work showcased in this book aims at participating in the endeavor. Indeed, it provides a collection of "sightings" that document and finally enable comparison of different cities.

Anyway, "The City at the End of the Underground" aims to go beyond the interest of professionals. It aims to share concern about the urban condition in the present age of urbanization and globalization.

1. "The Charter of European Planning" - The European Council of Spatial Planners. ECTP-CEU 2013.

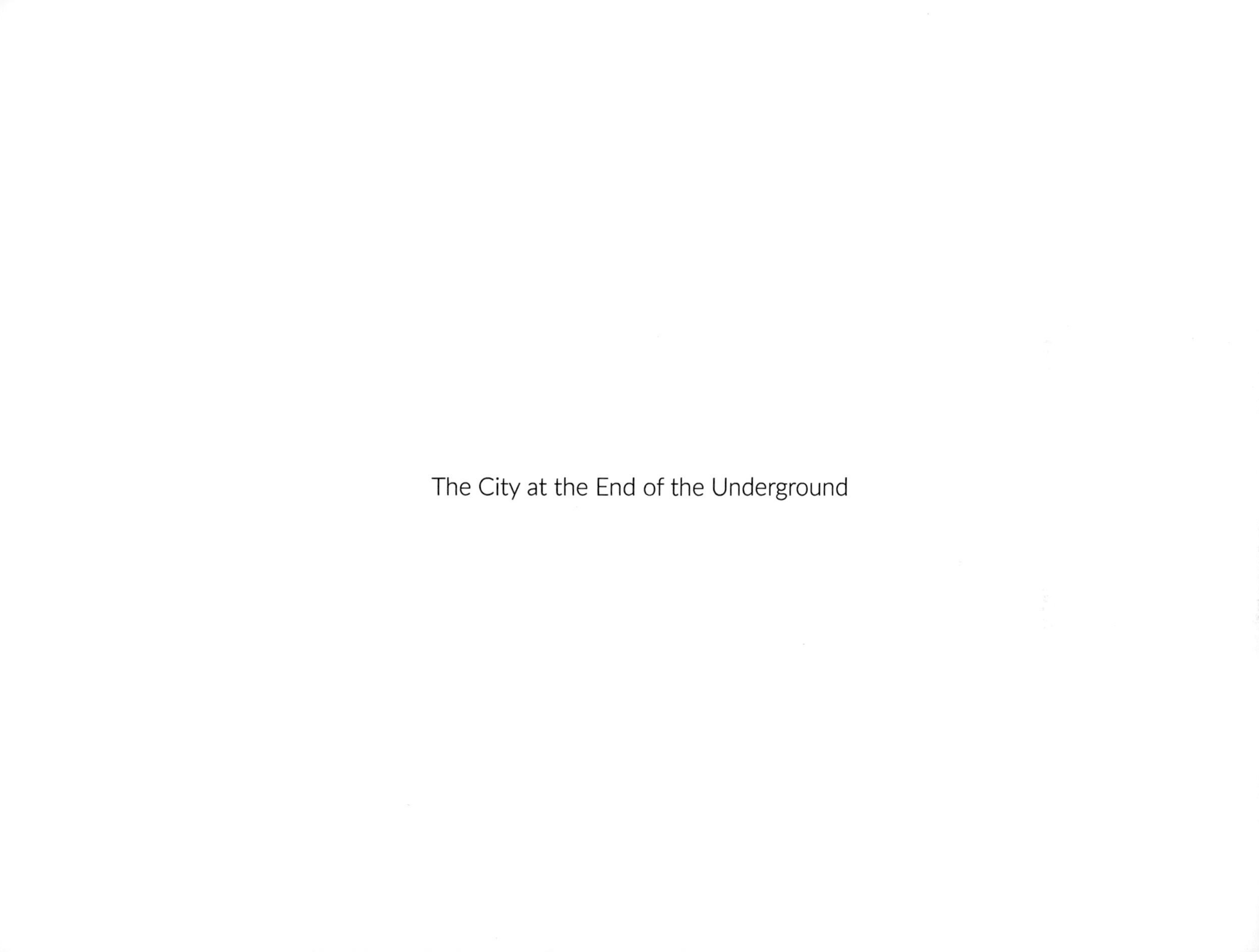

The City at the End of the Underground

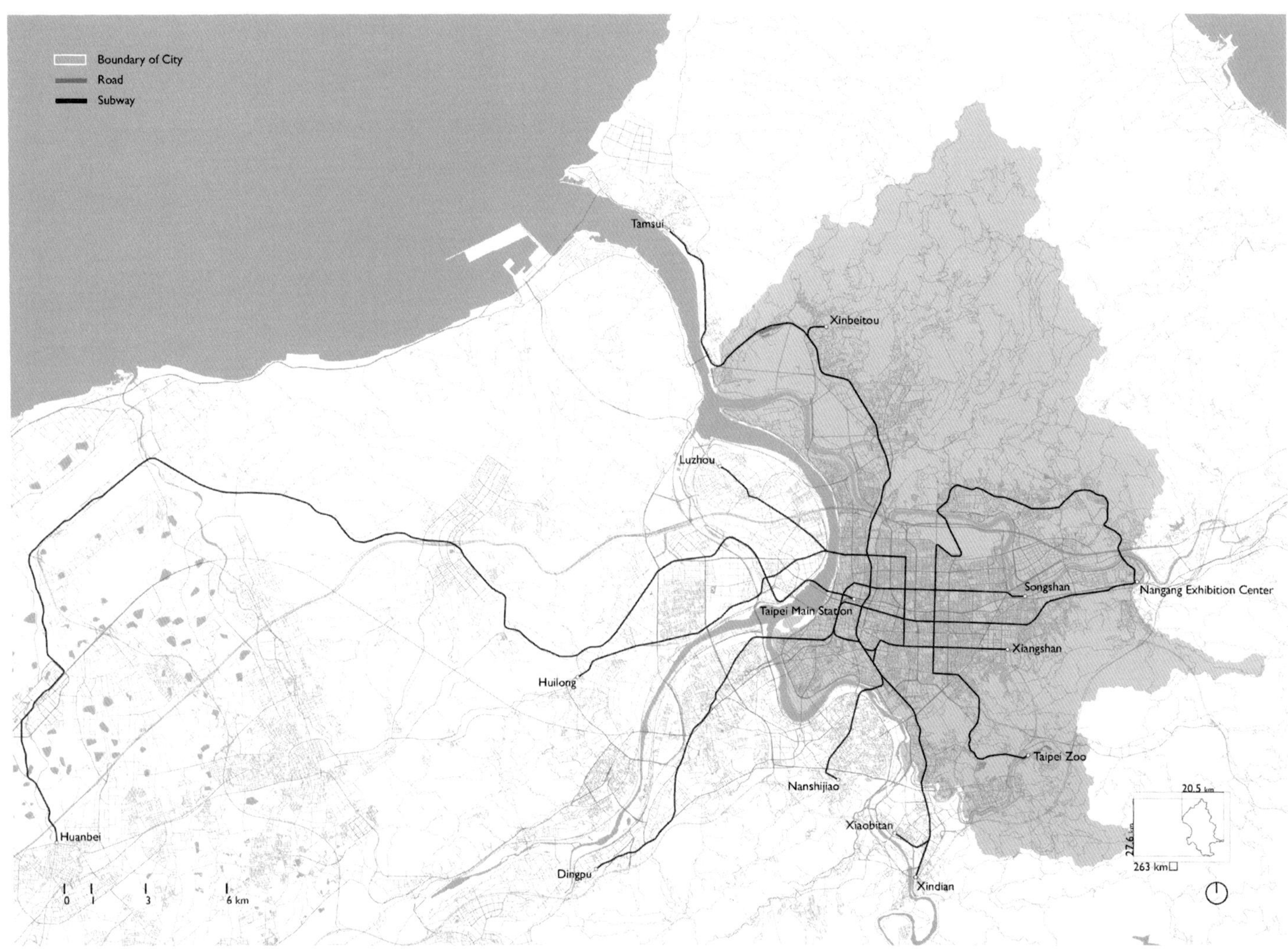
Boundary of City
Road
Subway
Tamsui
Xinbeitou
Luzhou
Songshan
Nangang Exhibition Center
Taipei Main Station
Xiangshan
Huilong
Taipei Zoo
Nanshijiao
Xiaobitan
Huanbei
Dingpu
Xindian
0 1 3 6 km
20.5 km
27.6 km
263 km□

Taipei Metro

operated by Taipei Rapid Transit Corporation (TRTC)

+

Taiwan Taoyuan International Airport Access MRT

operated by Taoyuan Metro Corporation

Line network: 131 km

Annual ridership: 717 millions*

* https://www.metro.taipei/, 2017

Terminal stations:

- Taipei Zoo, Nangang Exibition Center, Wenhu Line - Opened 1996
- Tamsui, Xiangshan, Tamsui-Xinyi Line - Opened 1997
- Xinbeitou, Xinbeitou Branch Line - Opened 1997
- Huilong, Luzhou, Nanshijiao, Zhonghe-Xinlu Line - Opened 1998
- Songshan, Xindian, Songshan-Xindian Line - Opened 1999
- Nangang Exibition Center, Dingpu, Bannan Line - Opened 1999
- Xiaobitan, Xiaobitan Branch Line - Opened 2004
- Taipei Main Station, Huanbei, Taoyuan Airport MRT Line - Opened 2017

In the following pages, the stations appear in counterclockwise order, starting from North.

16 Xinbeitou Station, Xinbeitou Branch Line

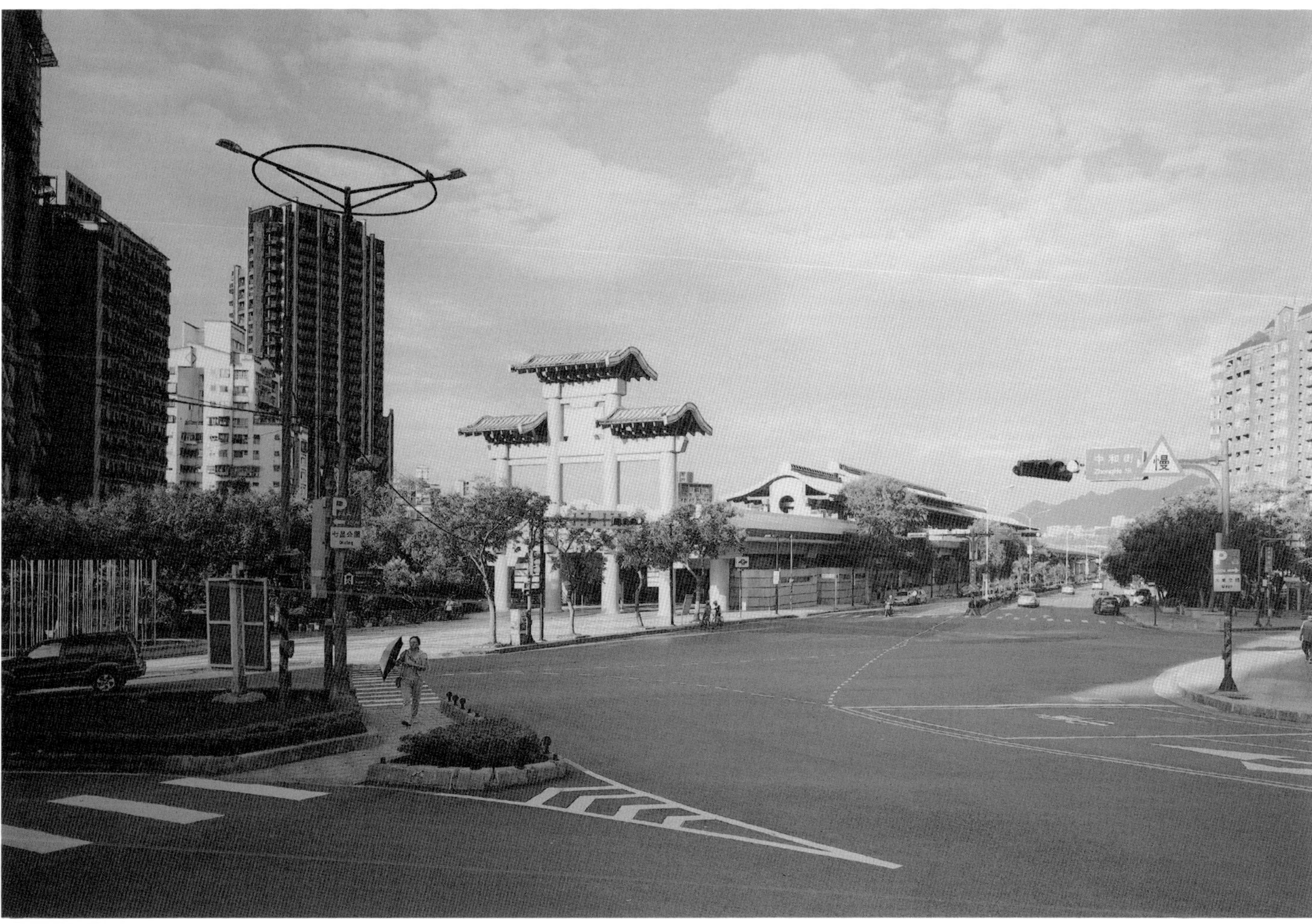
中和街
慢
P

18 Tamsui Station, Tamsui-Xinyi Line

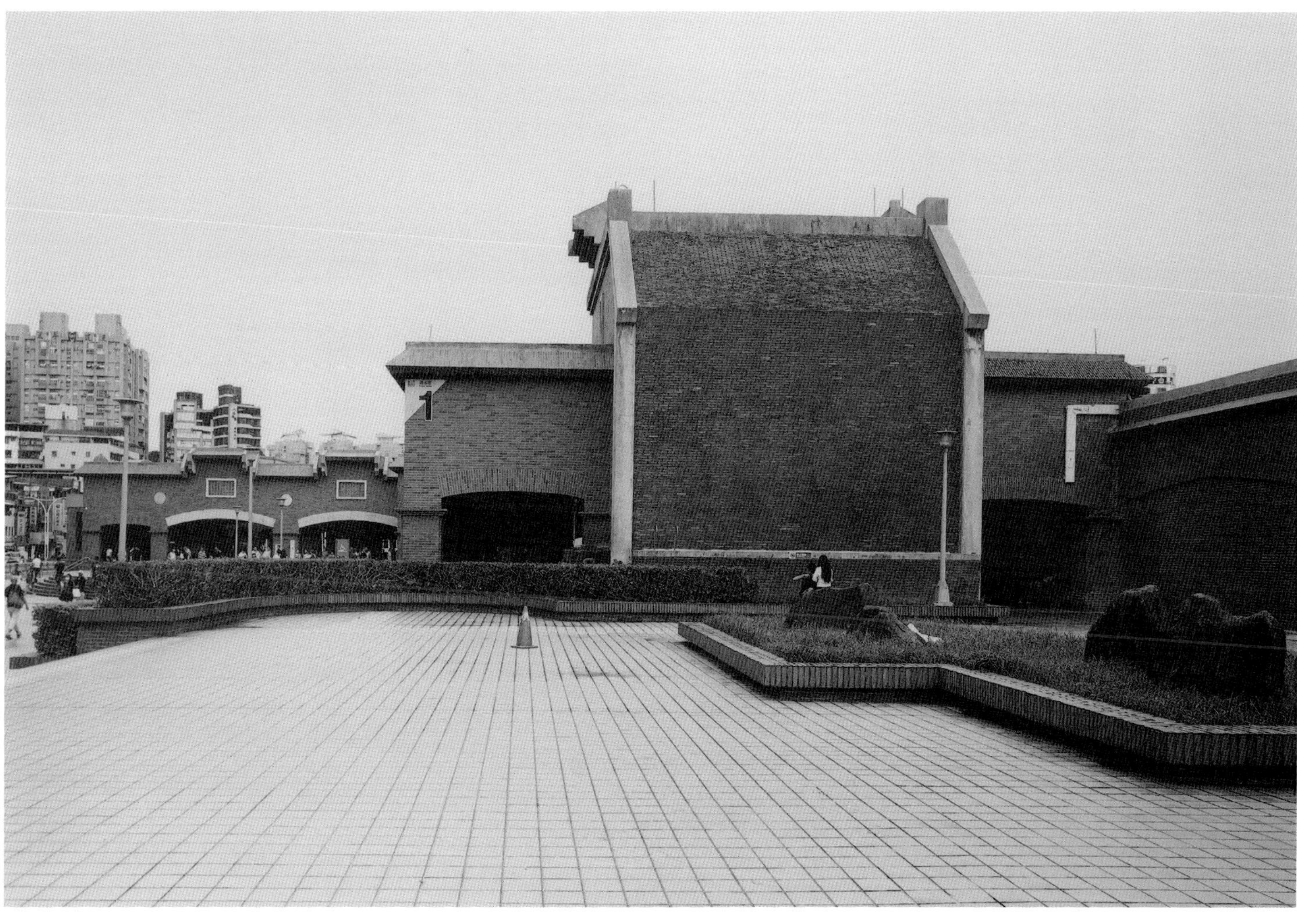
1

20 Luzhou Station, Zhonghe-Xinlu Line

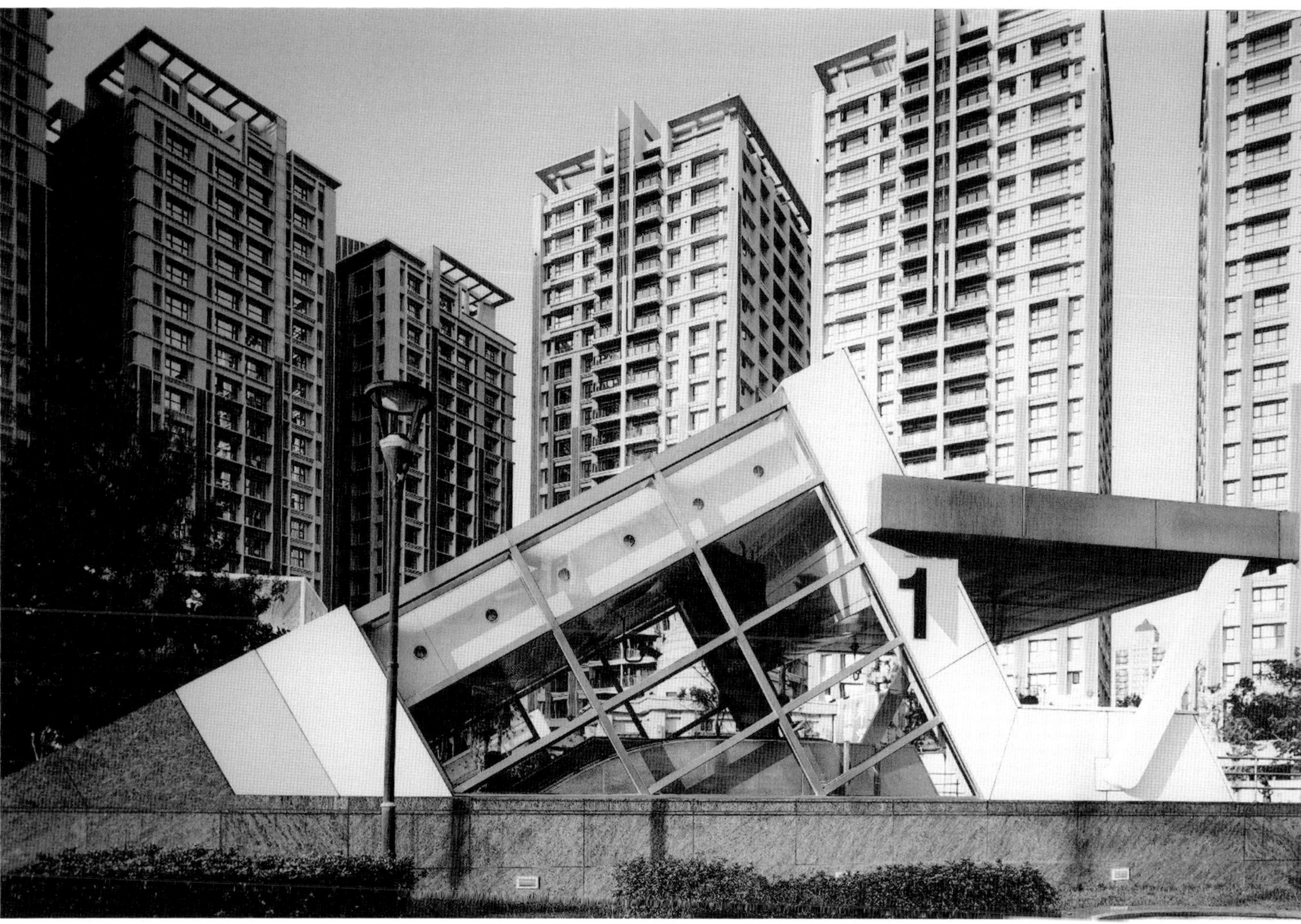
1

22 Huanbei Station, Taoyuan Airport MRT Line

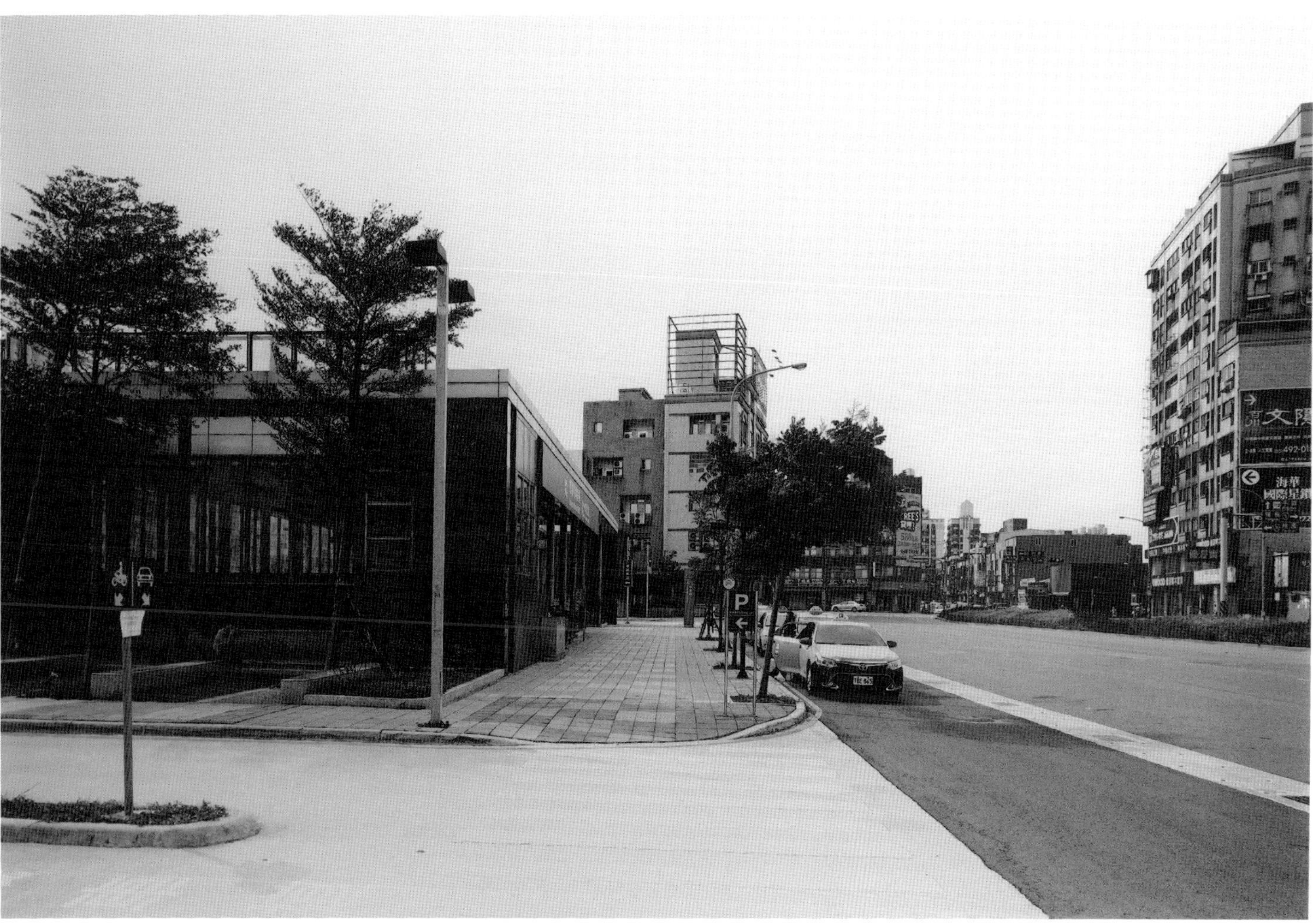
P
文
海華

24 Huilong Station, Zhonghe-Xinlu Line

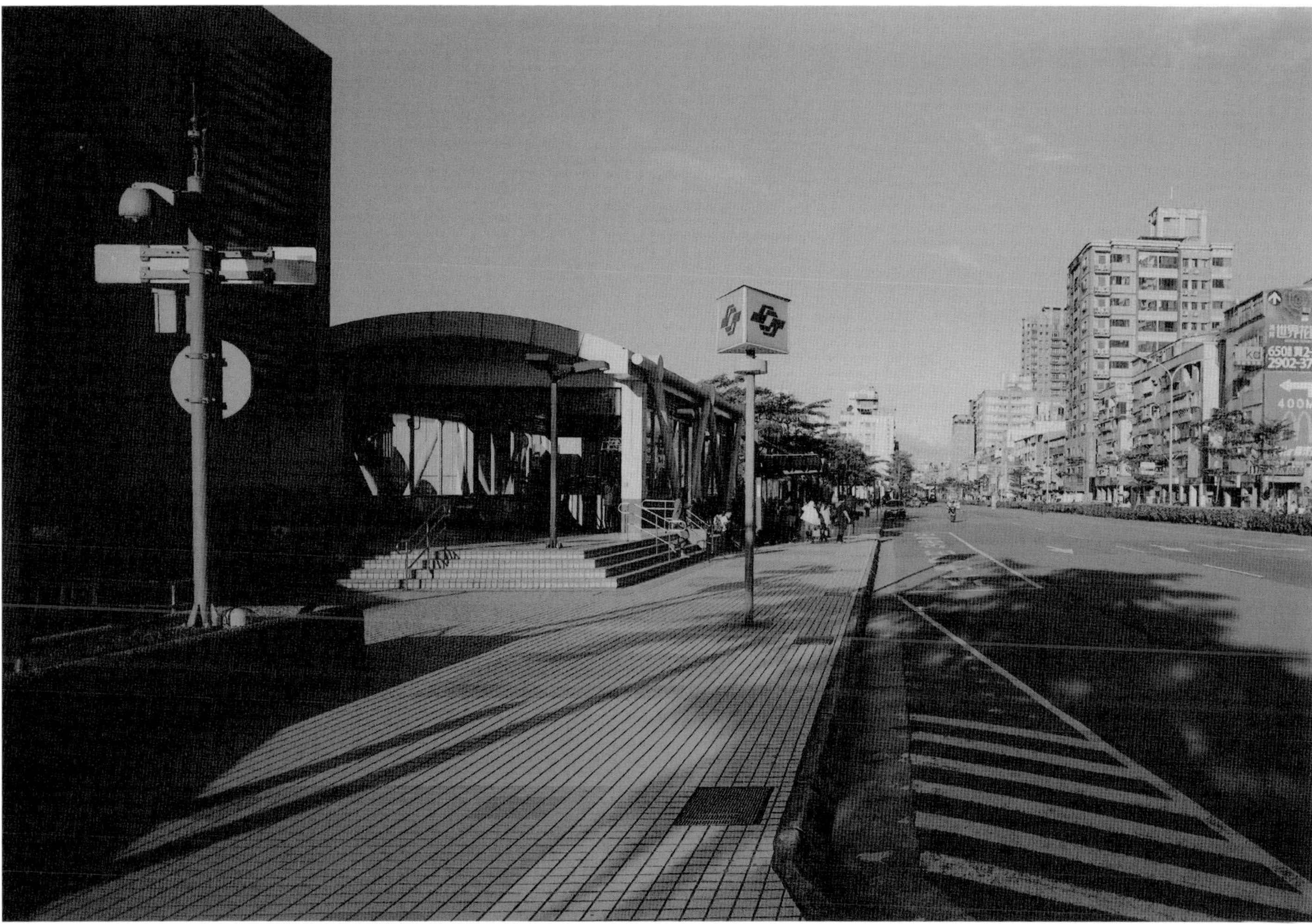
世界花
2902-378
400M

26 Dingpu Station, Bannan Line

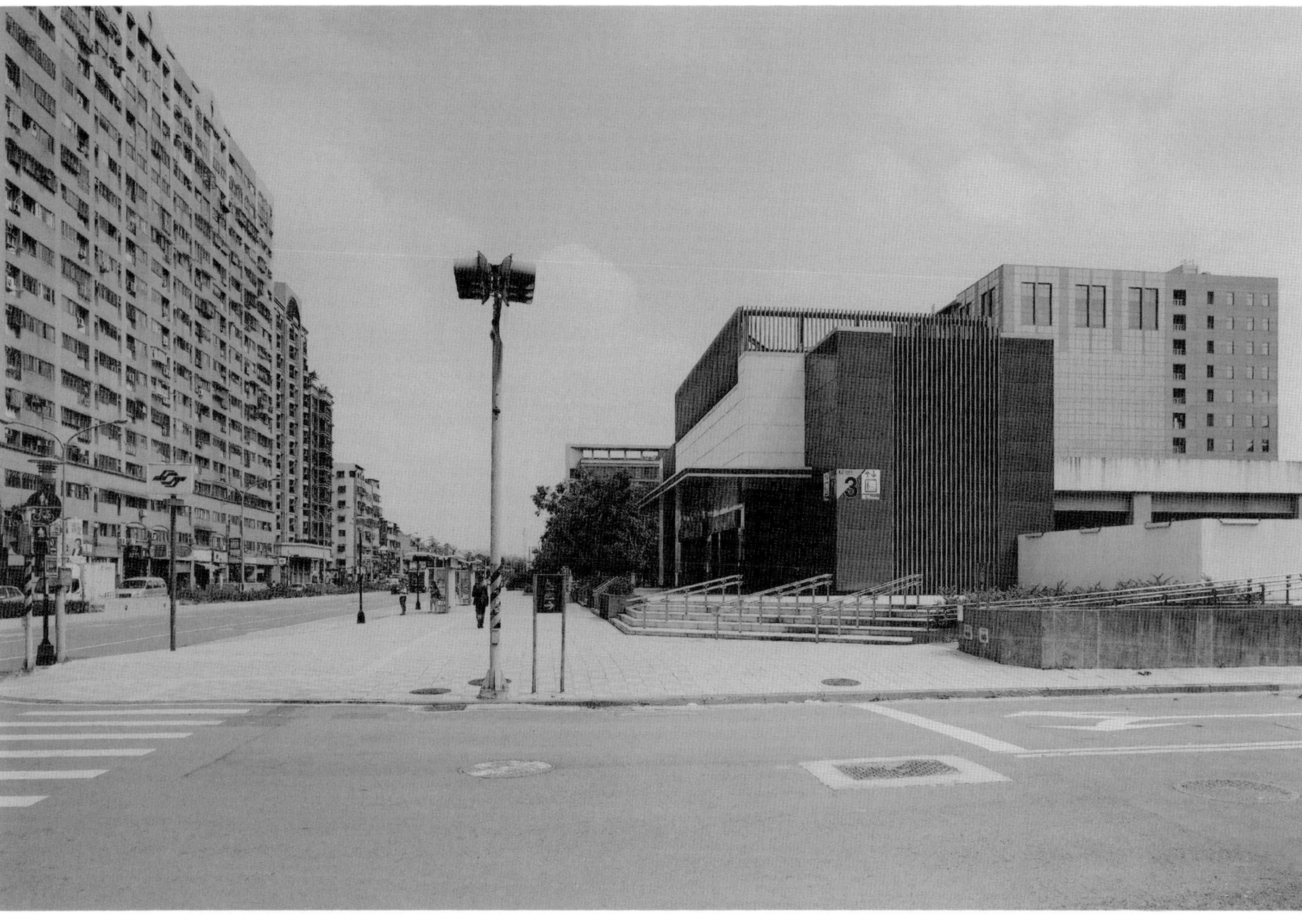
3

28 Nanshijiao Station, Zhonghe-Xinlu Line

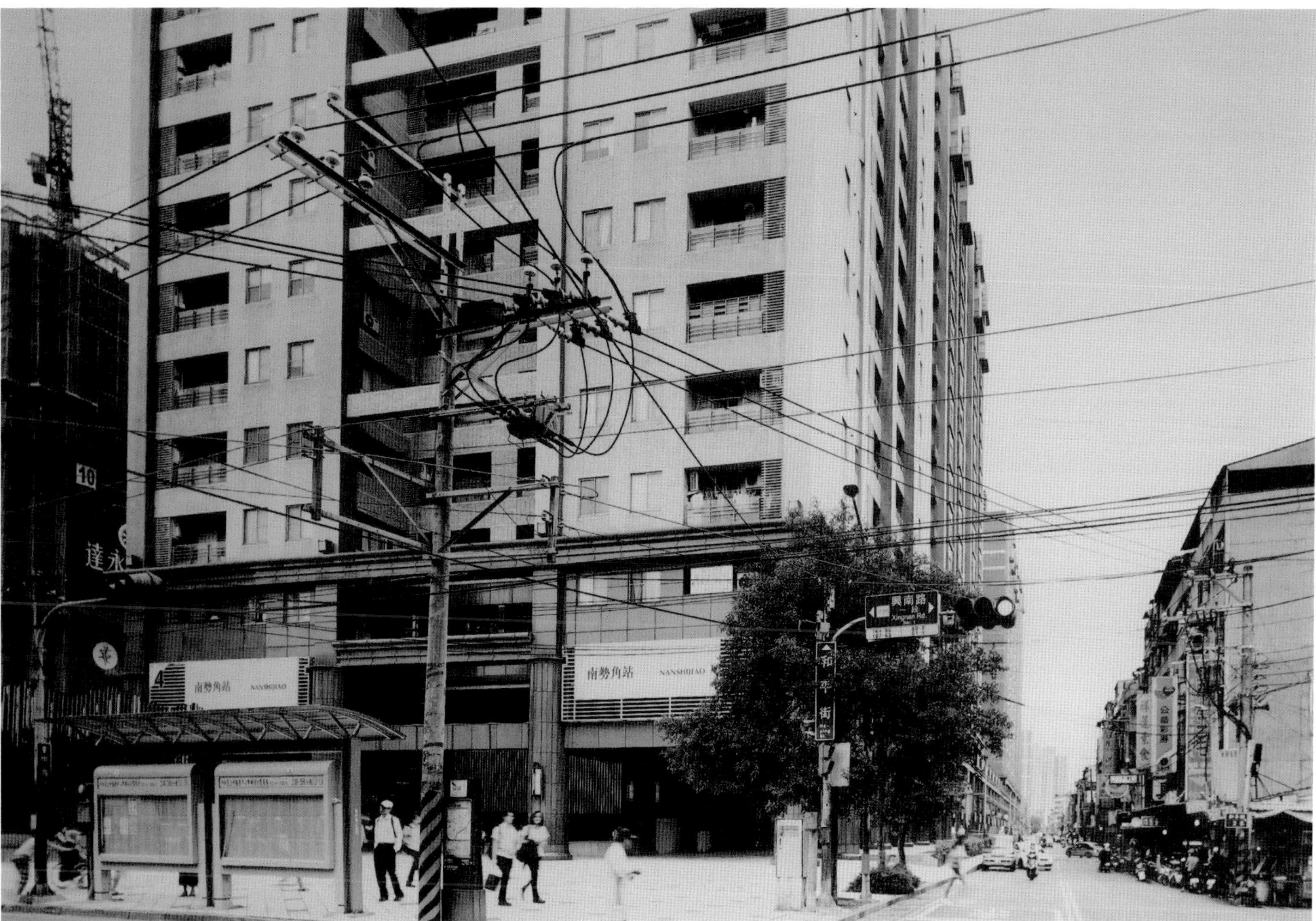
達永
南勢角站
NANSHIJIAO
南勢角站
NANSHIJIAO
興南路
和平街

30 Xiaobitan Station, Xiaobitan Branch Line

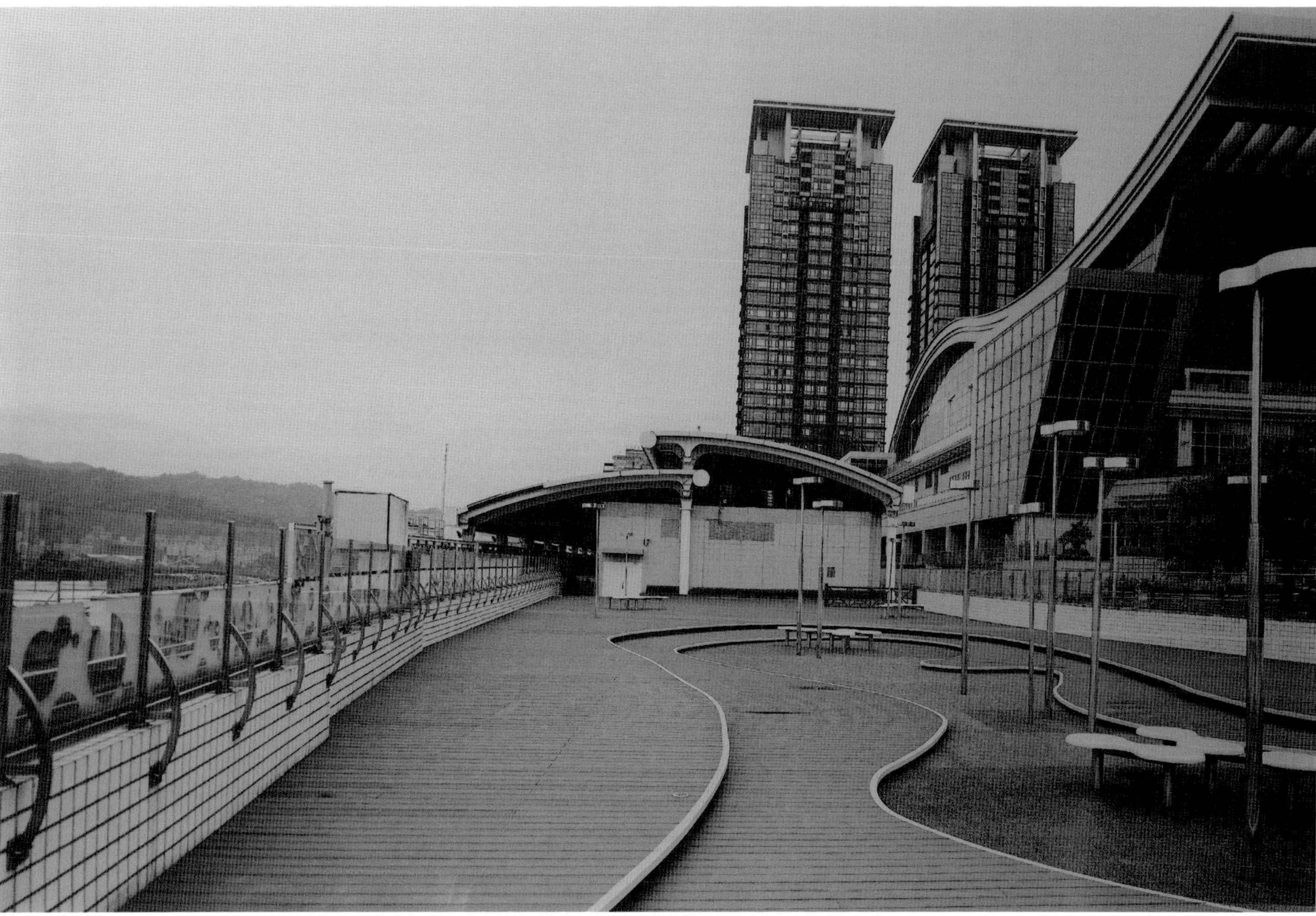

32 Xindian Station, Songshan-Xindian Line

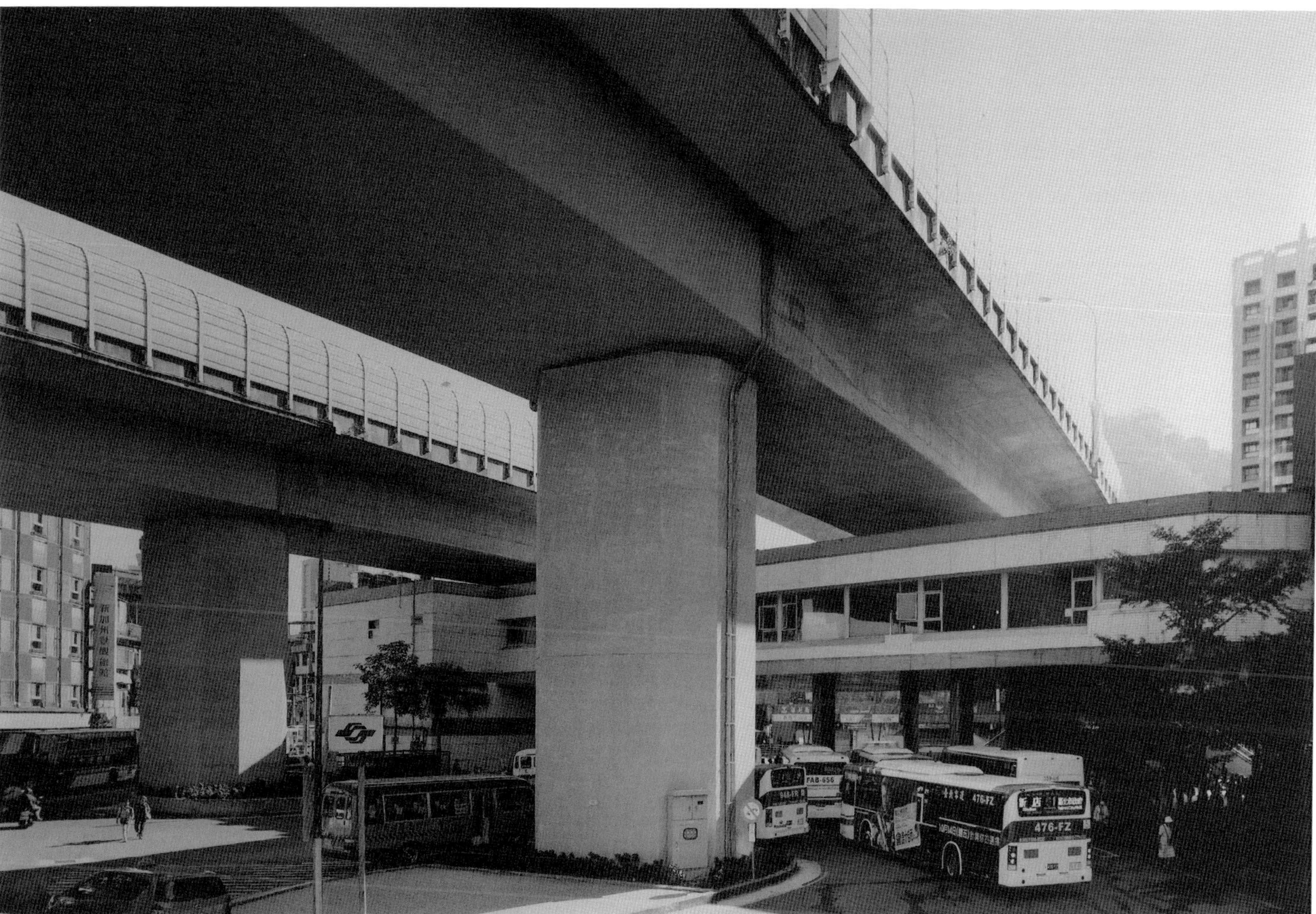
FAB-656
476-FZ
新店
476-FZ

34 Taipei Zoo Station, Wenhu Line

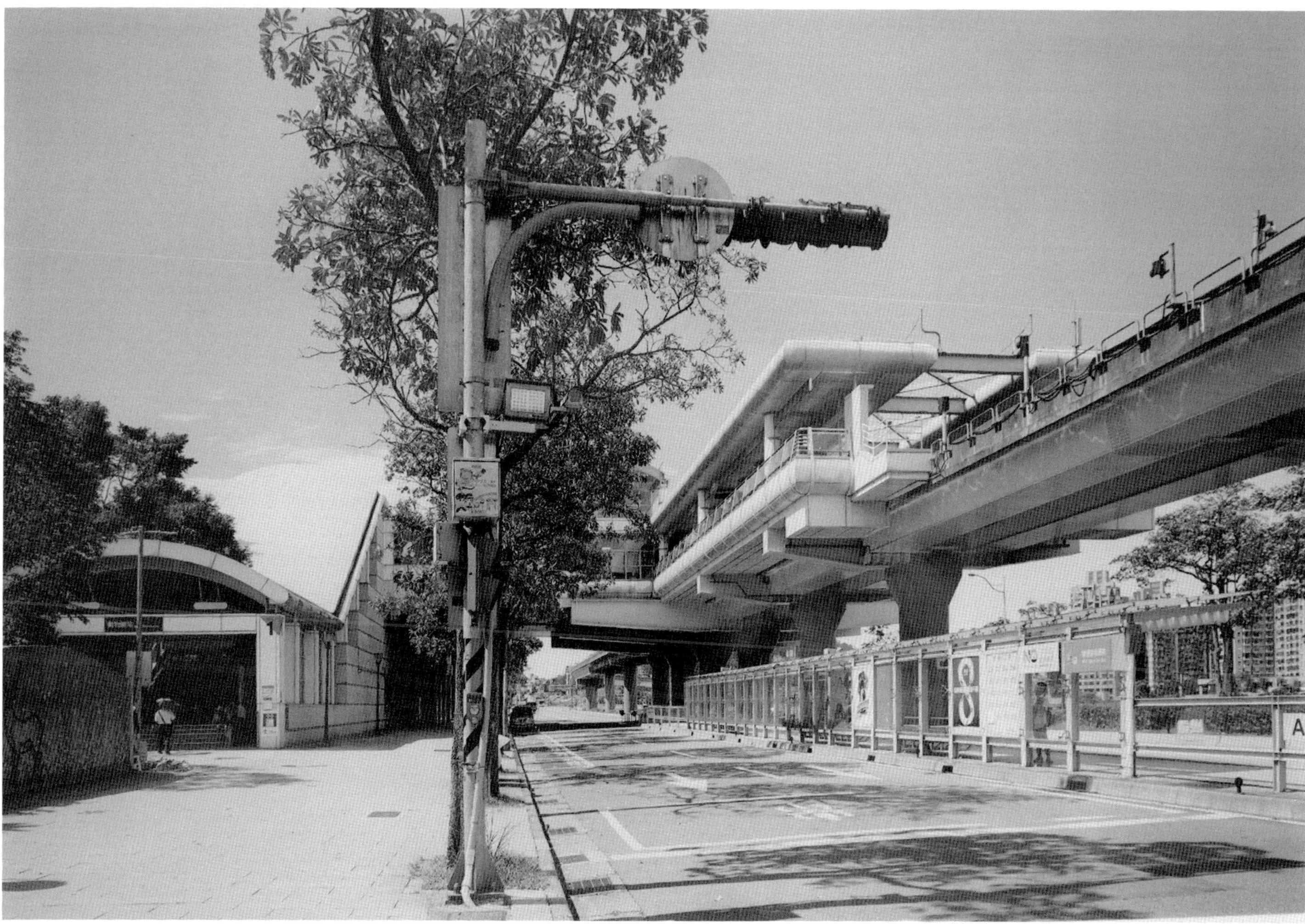

36 Xiangshan Station, Tamsui-Xinyi Line

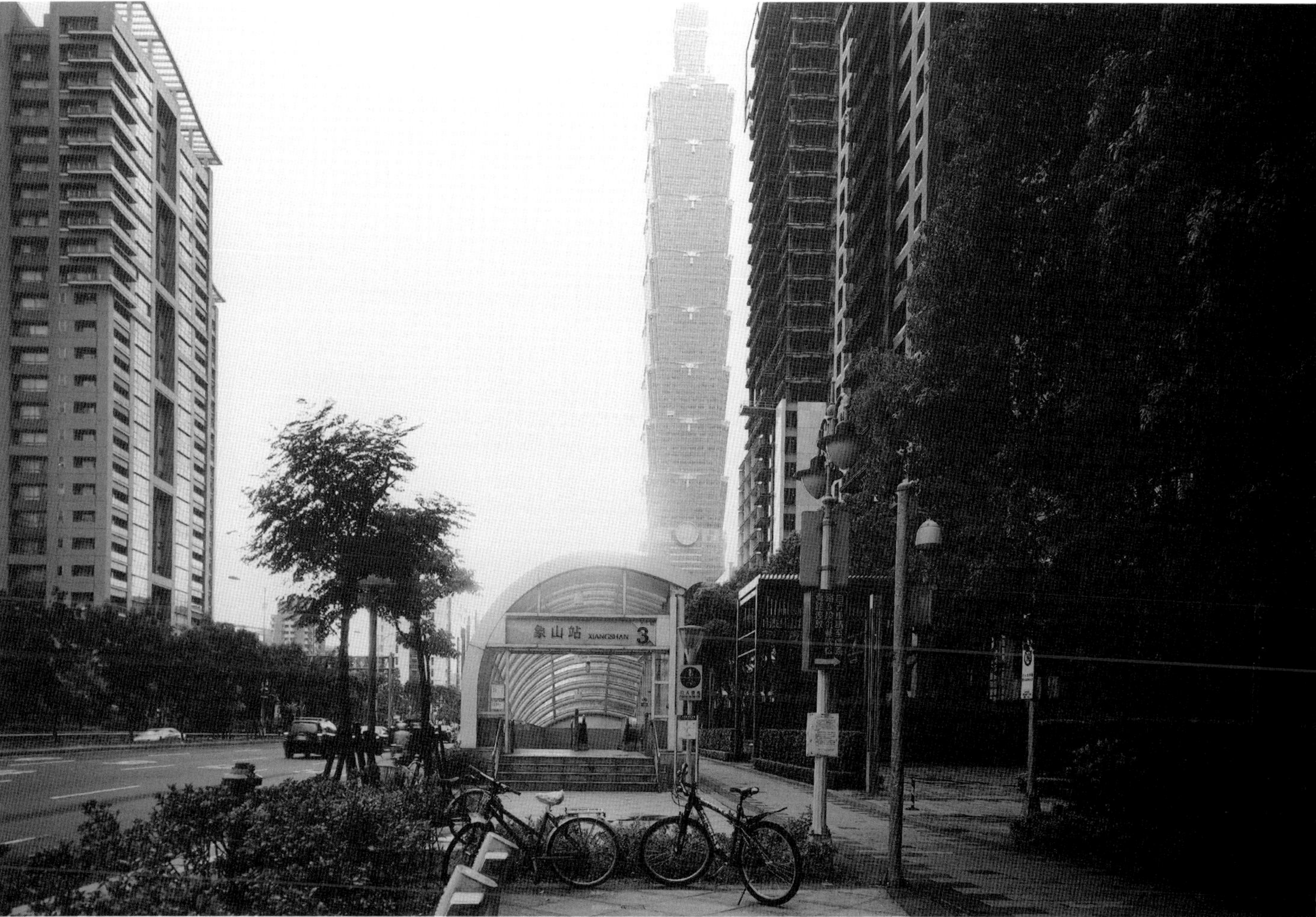
象山站 XIANGSHAN 3

38 Nangang Exhibition Center Station, Wenhu Line / Bannan Line

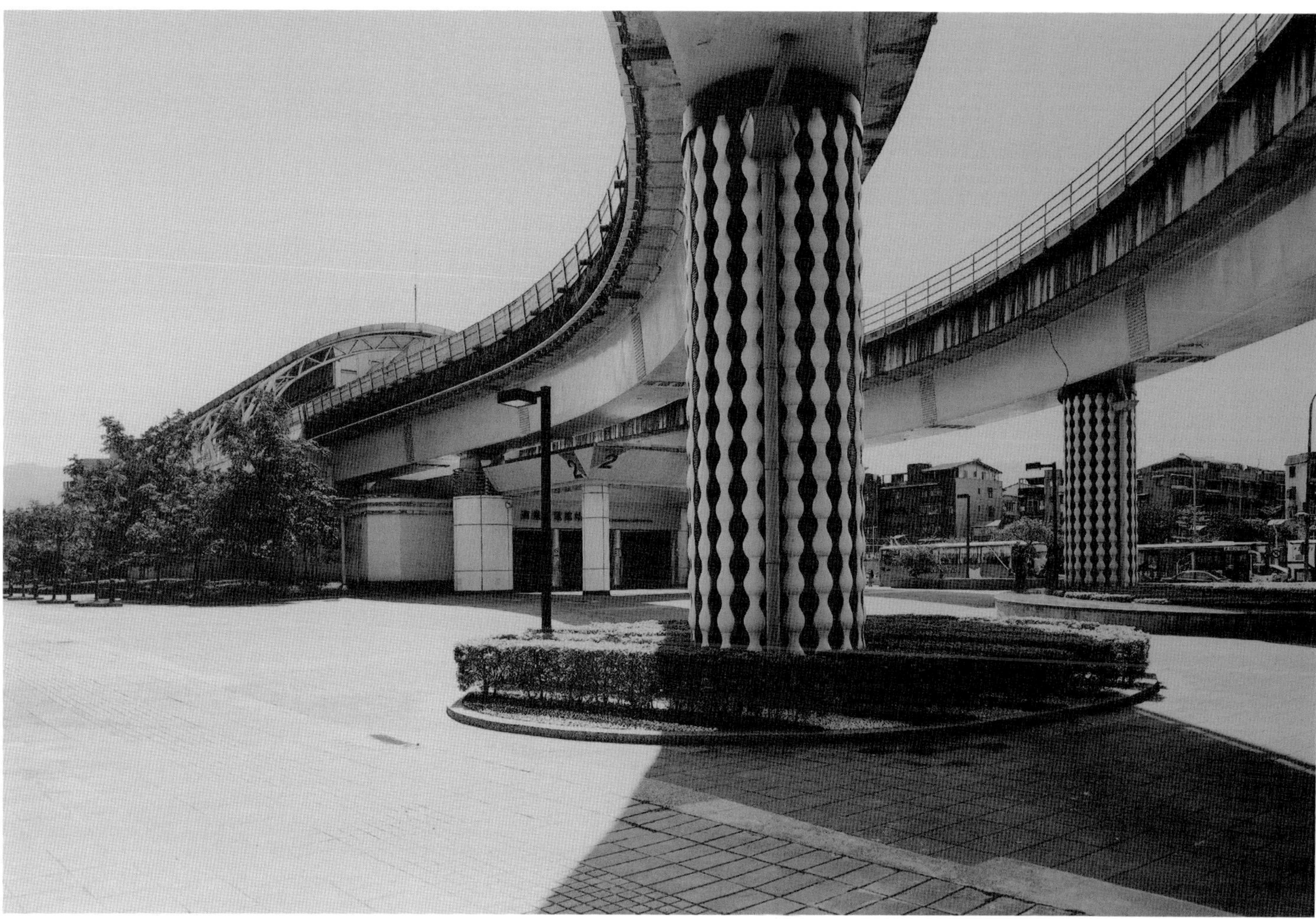

40 Songshan Station, Songshan-Xindian Line

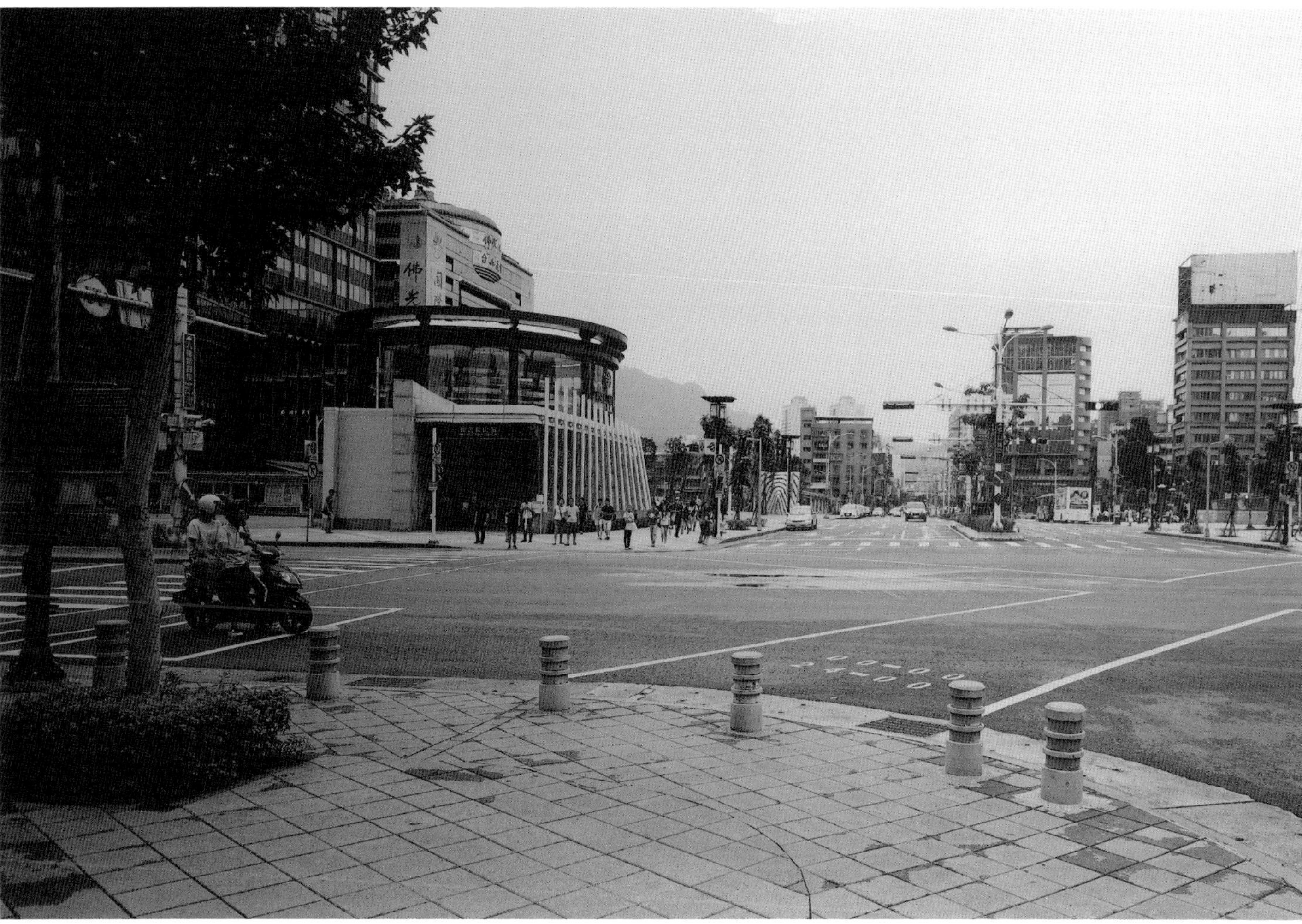

42 Taipei Main Station, Taoyuan Airport MRT Line

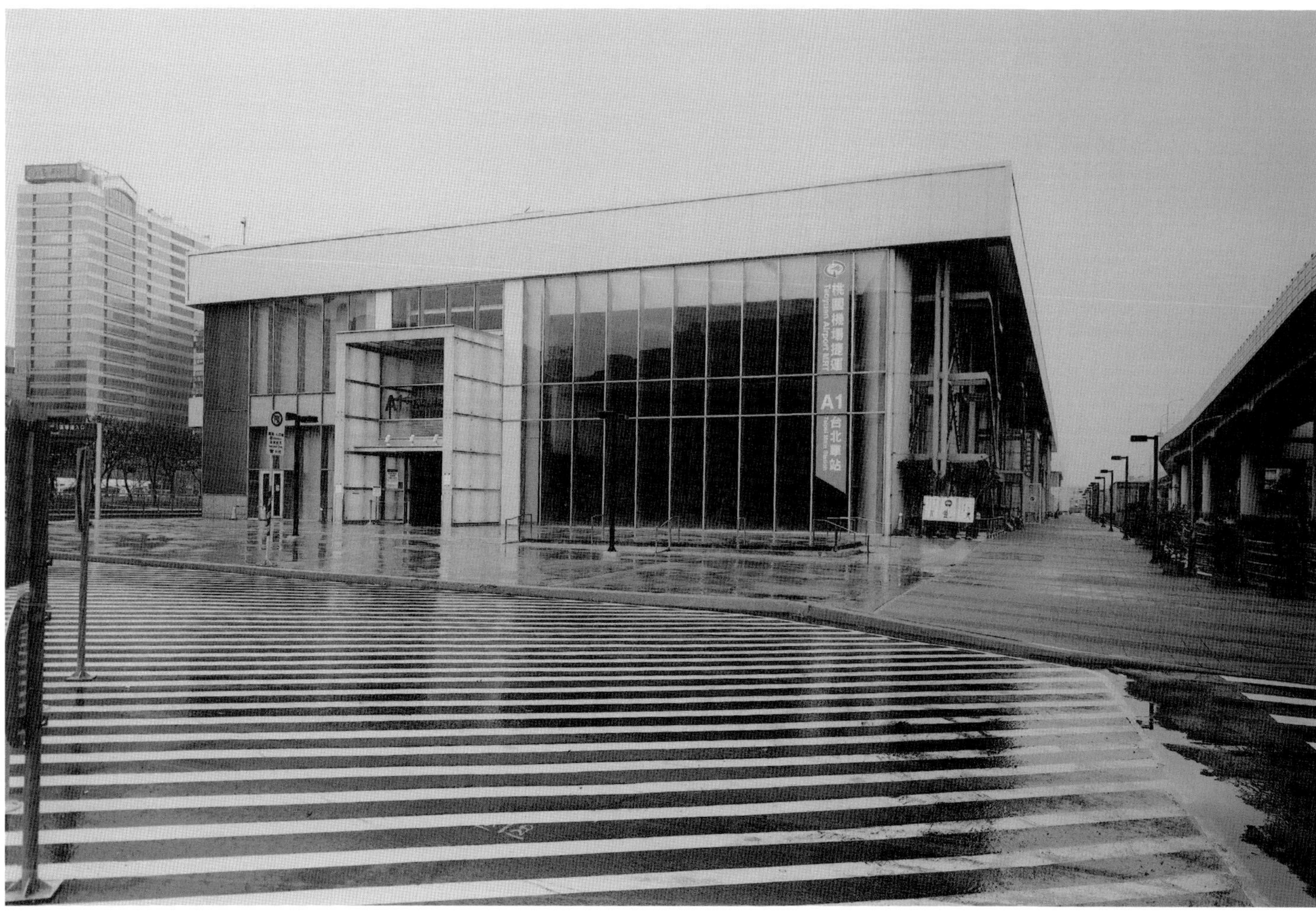
桃園機場捷運
Taoyuan Airport MRT
A1
台北車站

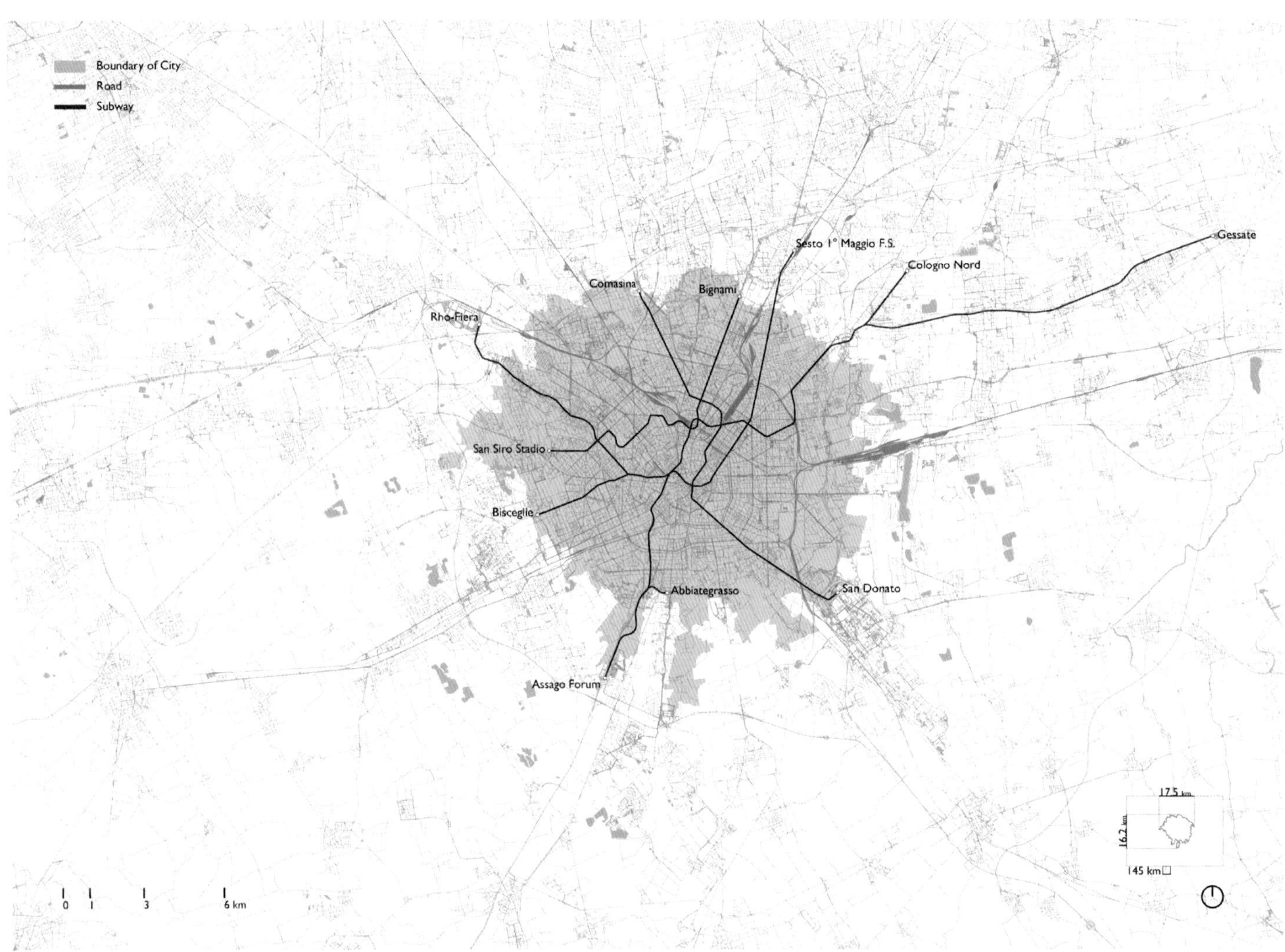
Boundary of City
Road
Subway
Gessate
Sesto 1° Maggio F.S.
Cologno Nord
Comasina
Bignami
Rho-Fiera
San Siro Stadio
Bisceglie
Abbiategrasso
San Donato
Assago Forum
17.5 km
16.2 km
145 km□
0
1
3
6 km

Metropolitana di Milano

Operated by Azienda Trasporti Milanesi (ATM)

Line network: 96.8 km
Annual ridership: 285 million*

* https://www.atm.it/, 2017

Terminal Stations:

- Bisceglie, Rho Fieramilano, Sesto 1° Maggio F.S., M1 Line - Opened 1964
- Assago Milanofiori Forum, P.za Abbiategrasso, Cologno Nord, Gessate, M2 Line - Opened 1969
- Comasina, San Donato, M3 Line - Opened 2011
- Bignami Parco Nord, San Siro Stadio, M5 Line - Opened 2013

In the following pages, the stations appear in counterclockwise order, starting from North.

46 Comasina Station, M3 Line

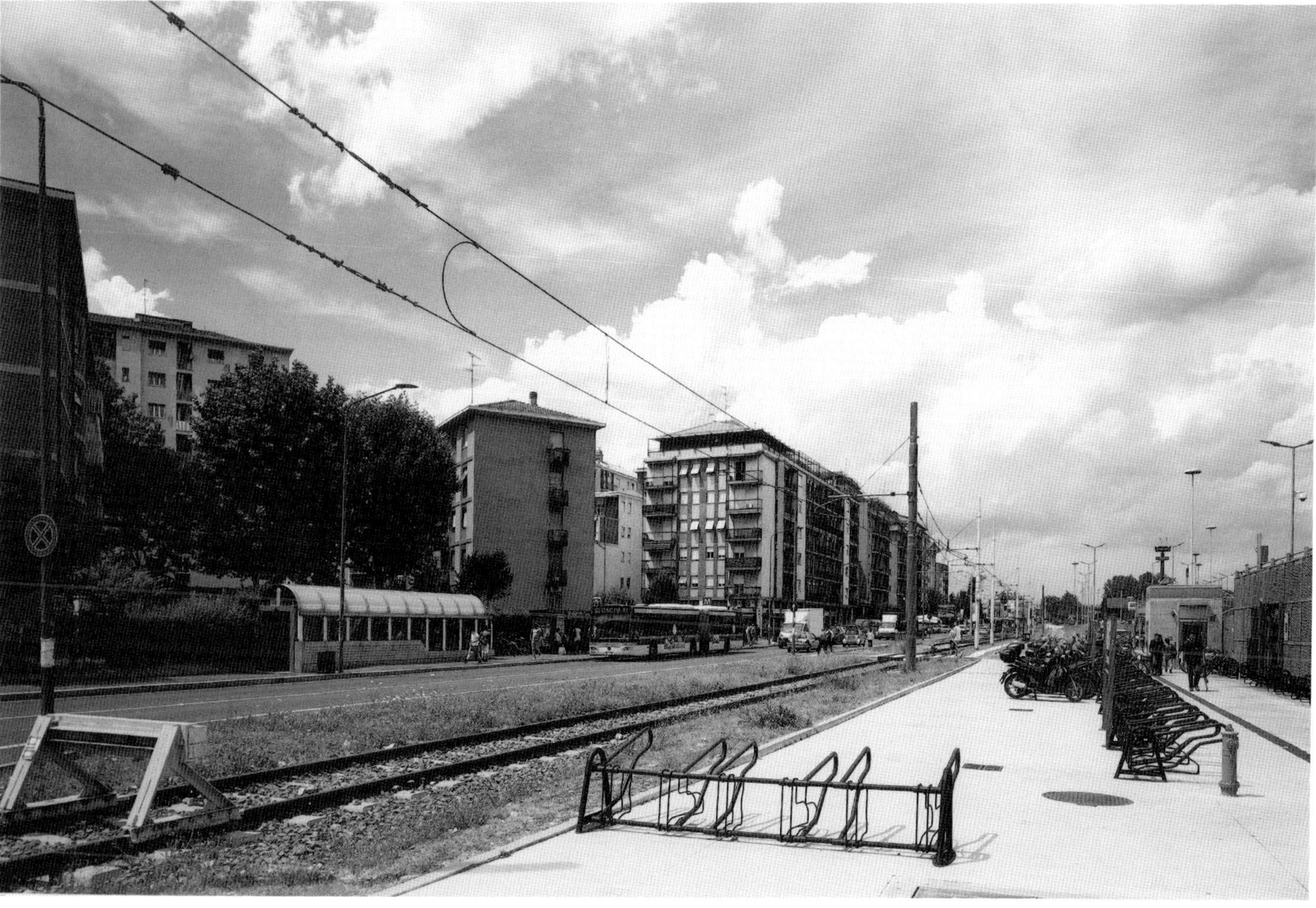

48 Rho Fieramilano Station, M1 Line

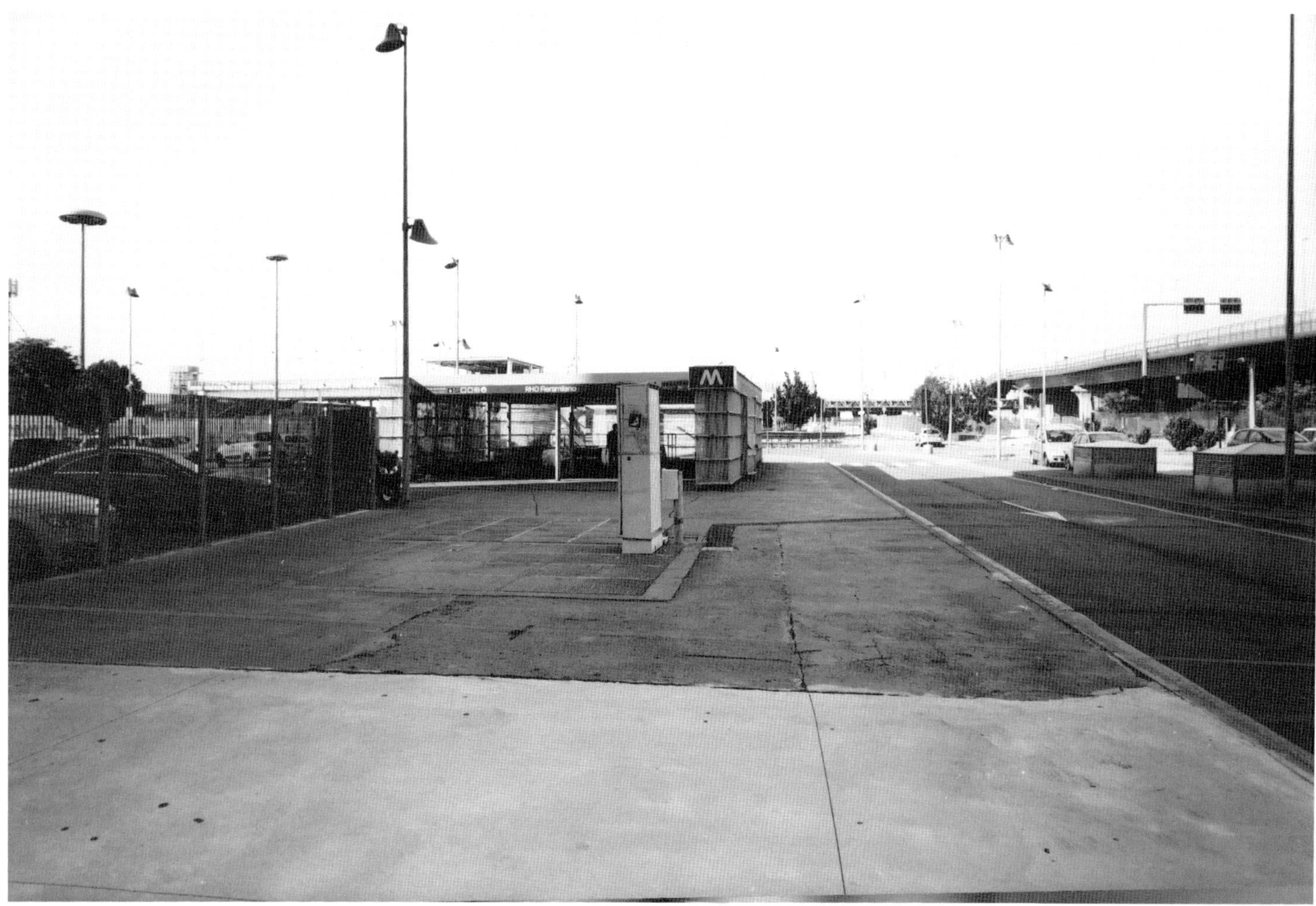

RHO Fieramilano
M

50 San Siro Stadio Station, M5 Line

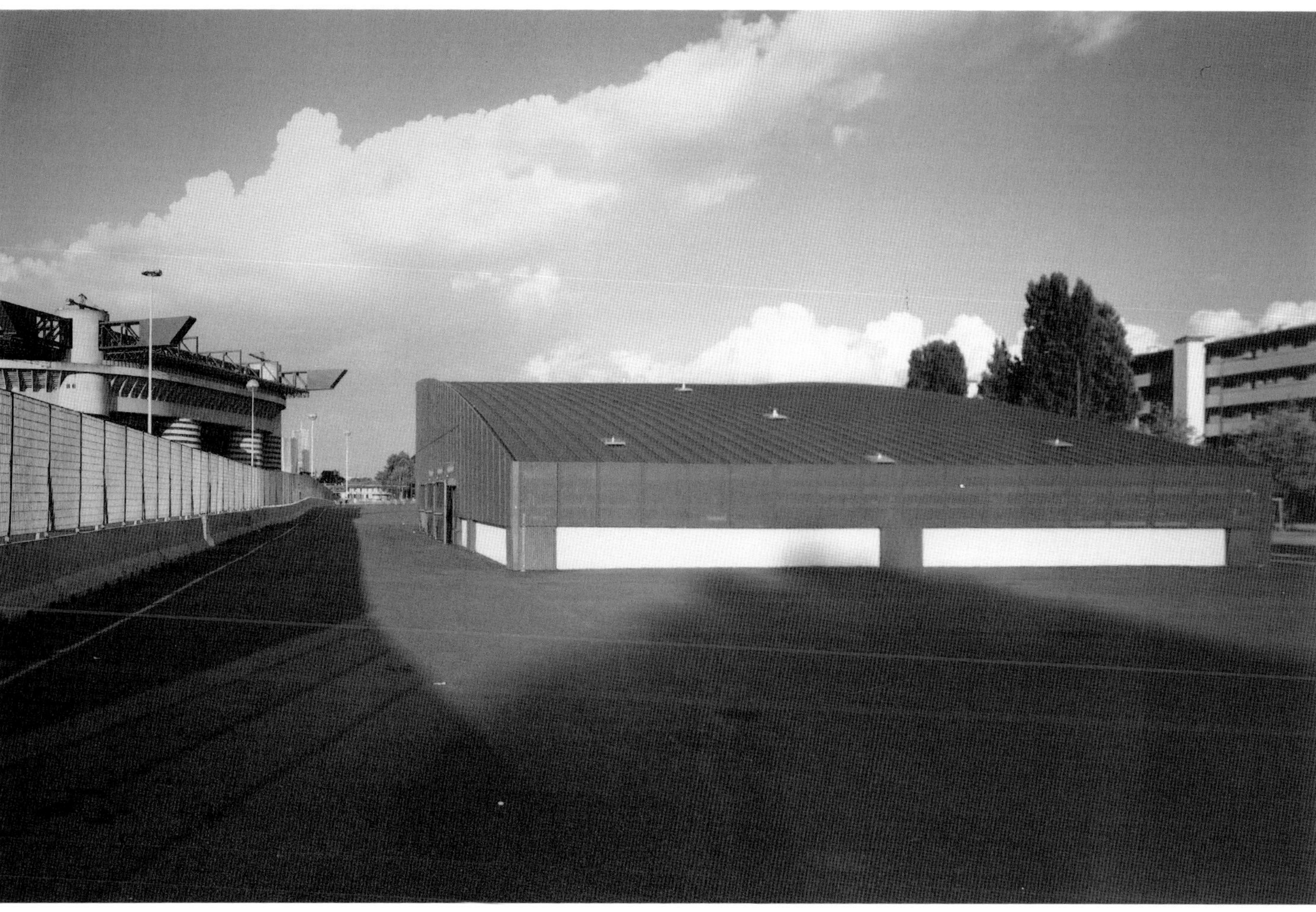

52 Bisceglie Station, M1 Line

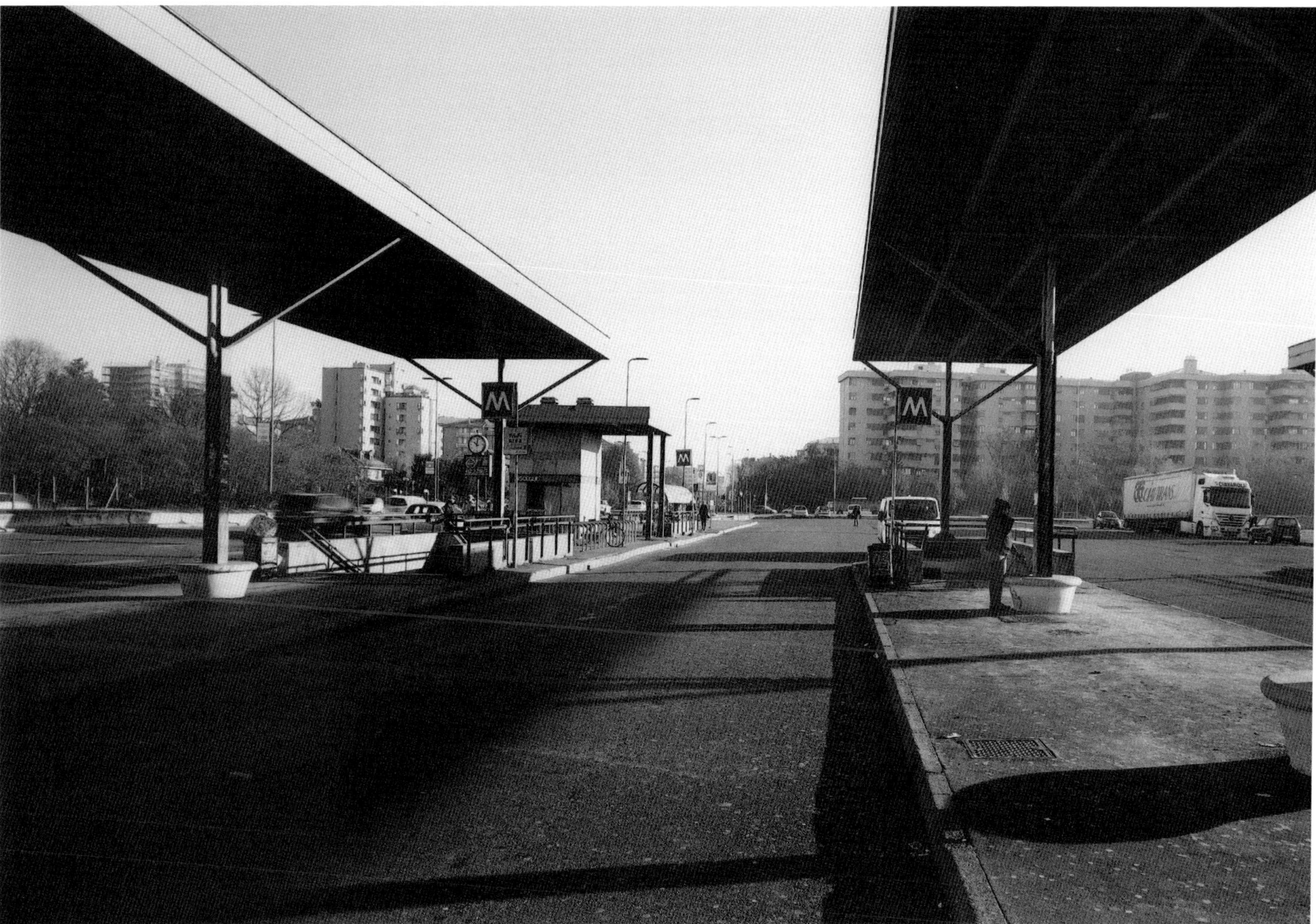

54 Assago Milanofiori Forum Station, M2 Line

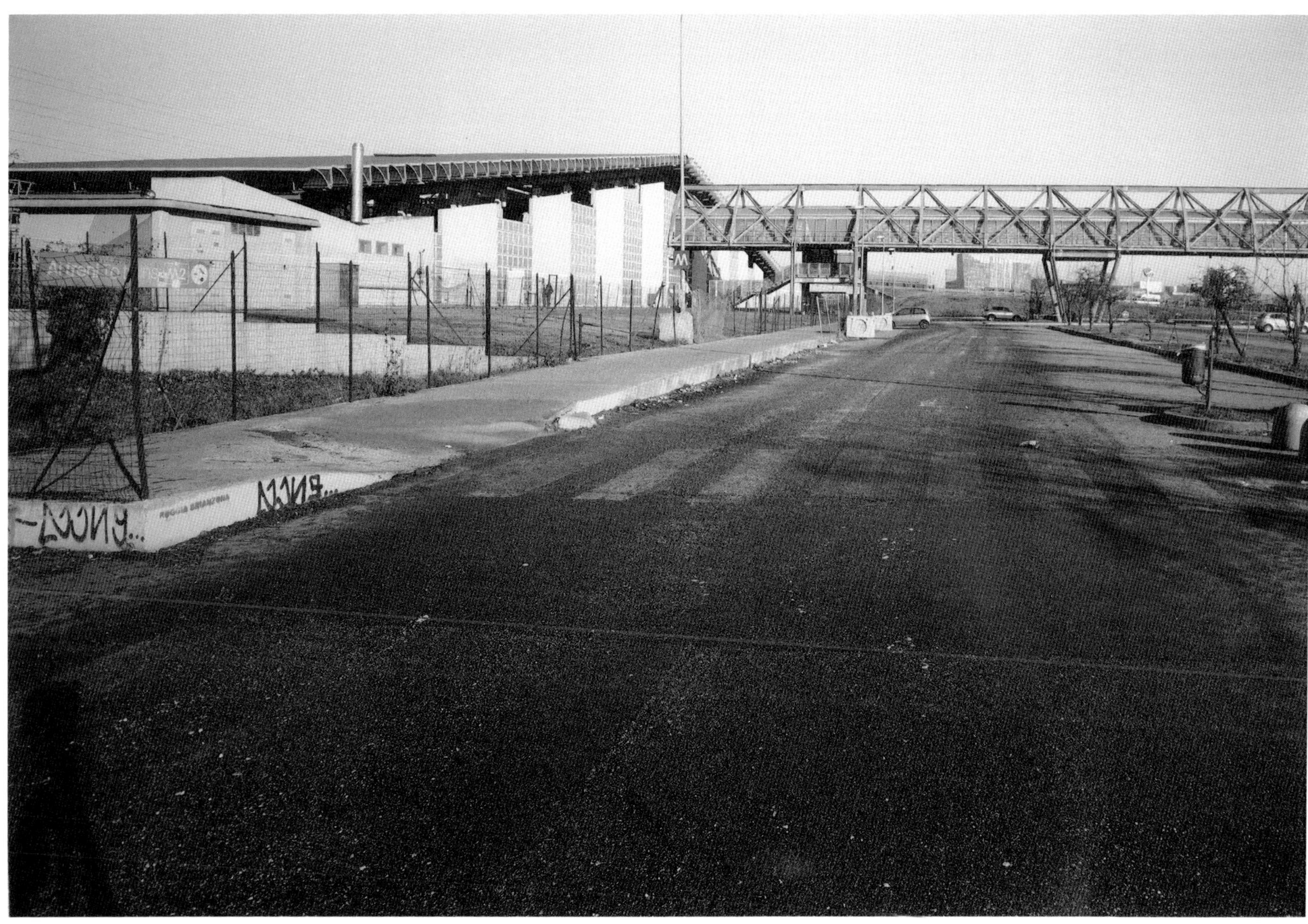

56 P.za Abbiategrasso Station, M2 Line

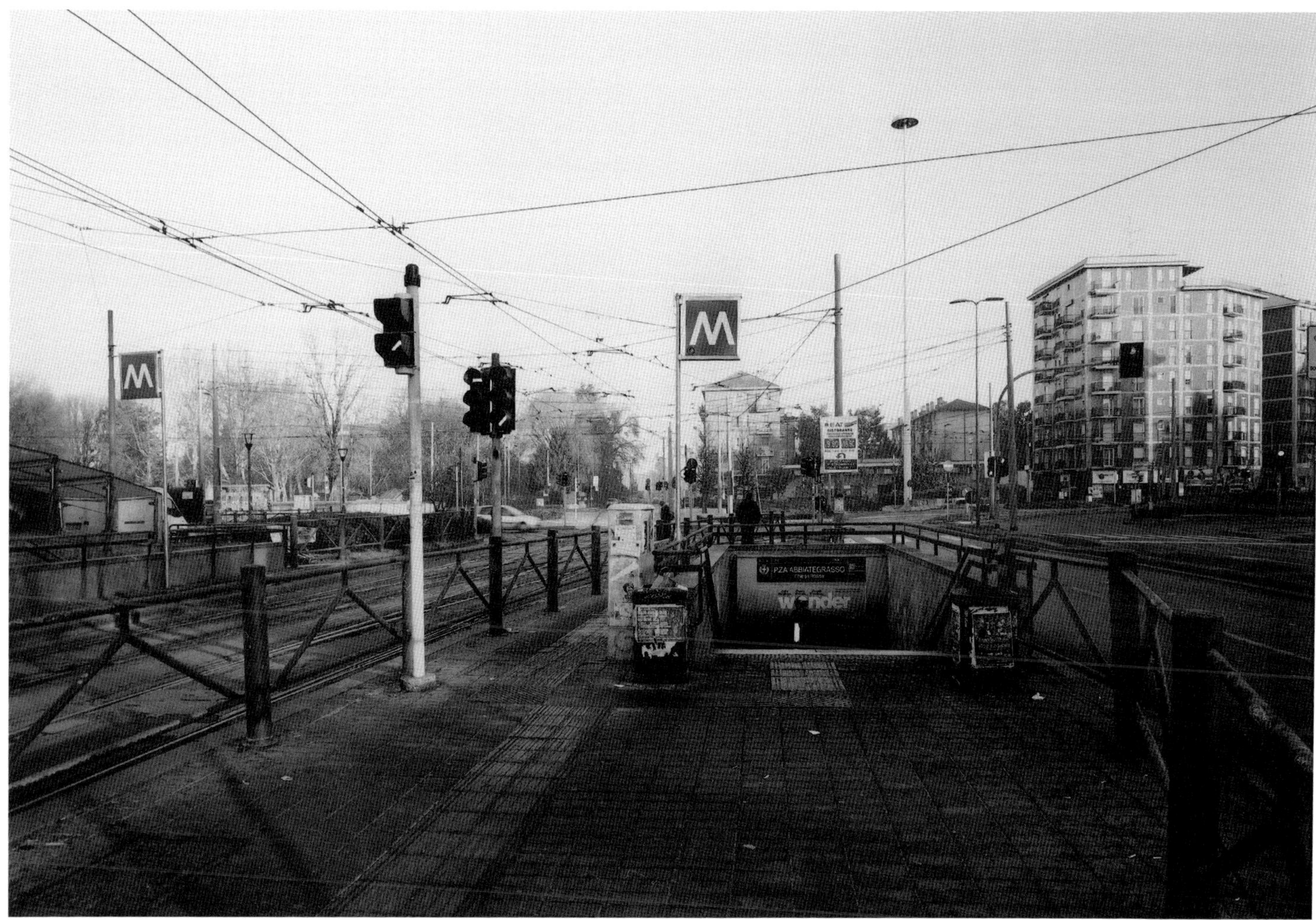
M
M
M
PZA ABBIATEGRASSO

58 San Donato Station, M3 Line

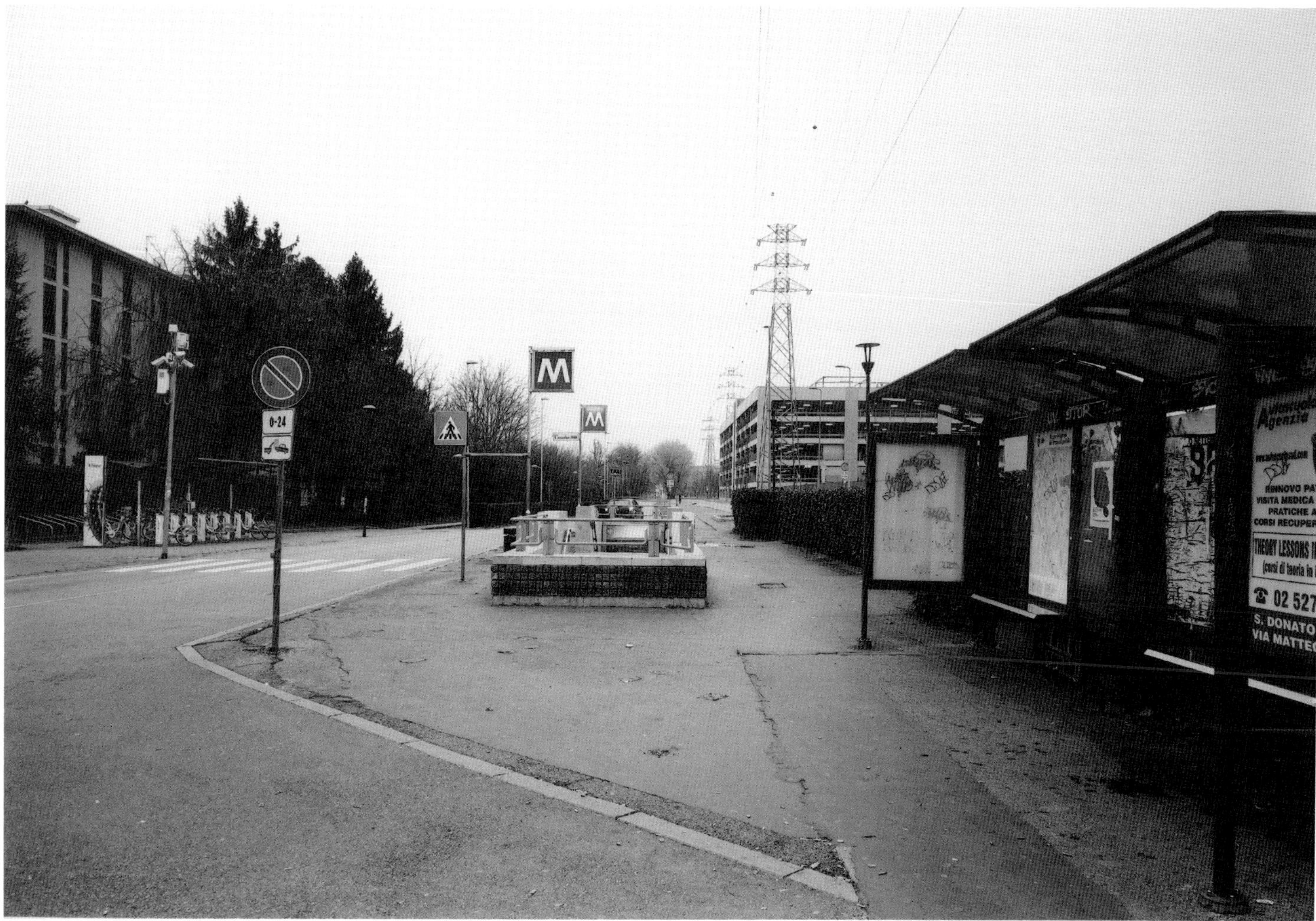
0-24
M
M
S. DONATO

60 Gessate Station, M2 Line

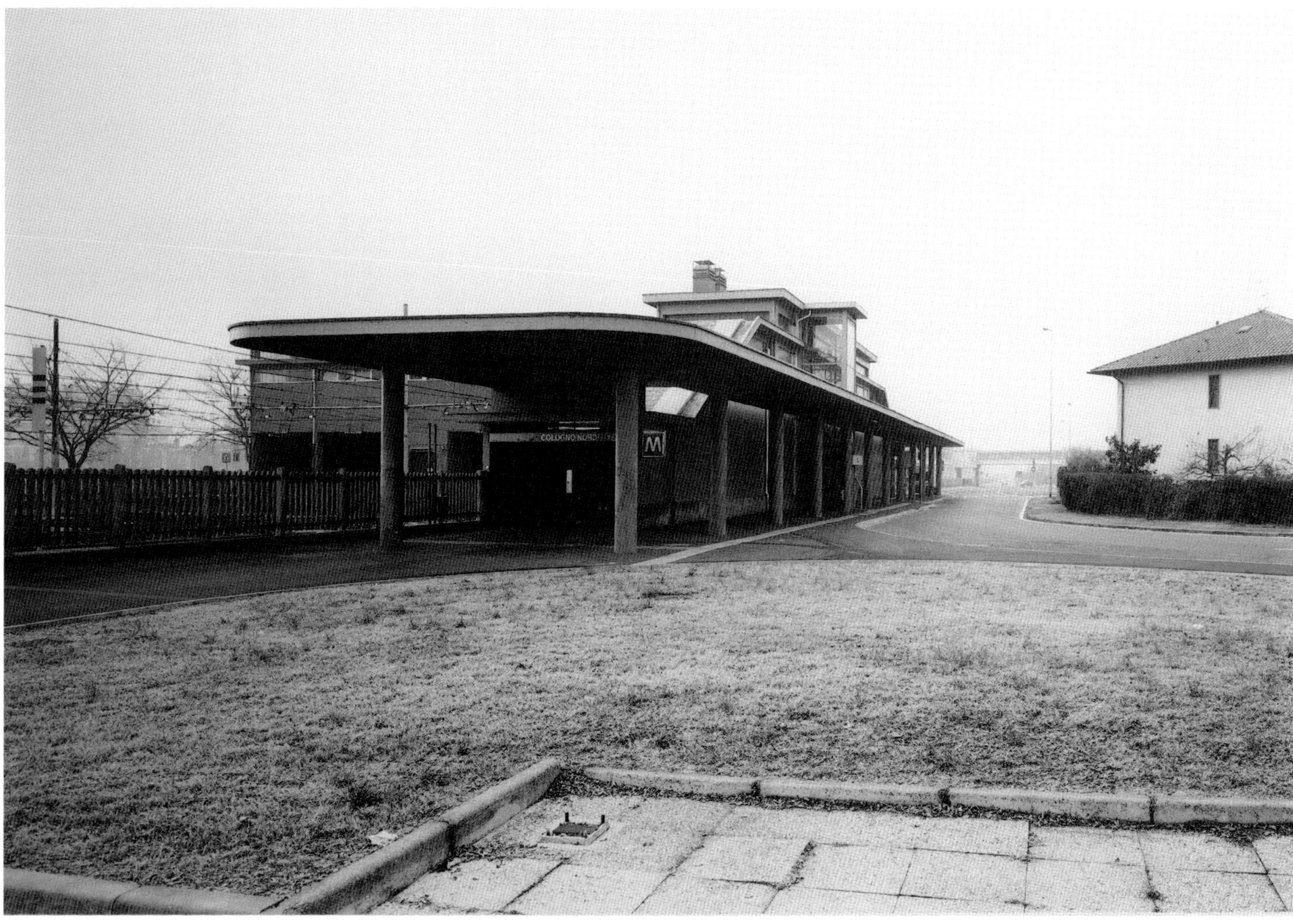
COLOGNO NORD
M

62 Cologno Nord Station, M2 Line

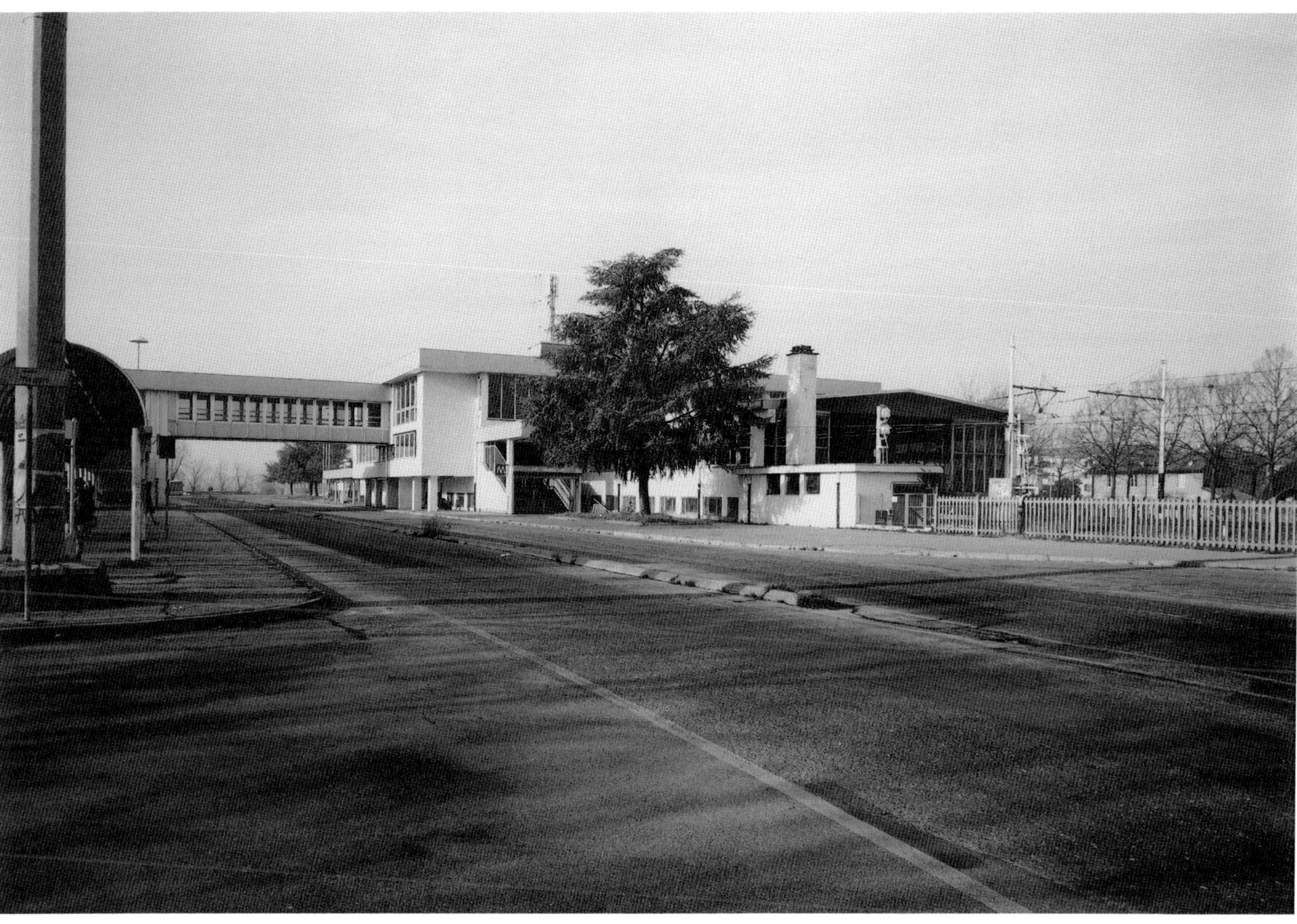

64 Sesto 1° Maggio F.S. Station, M1 Line

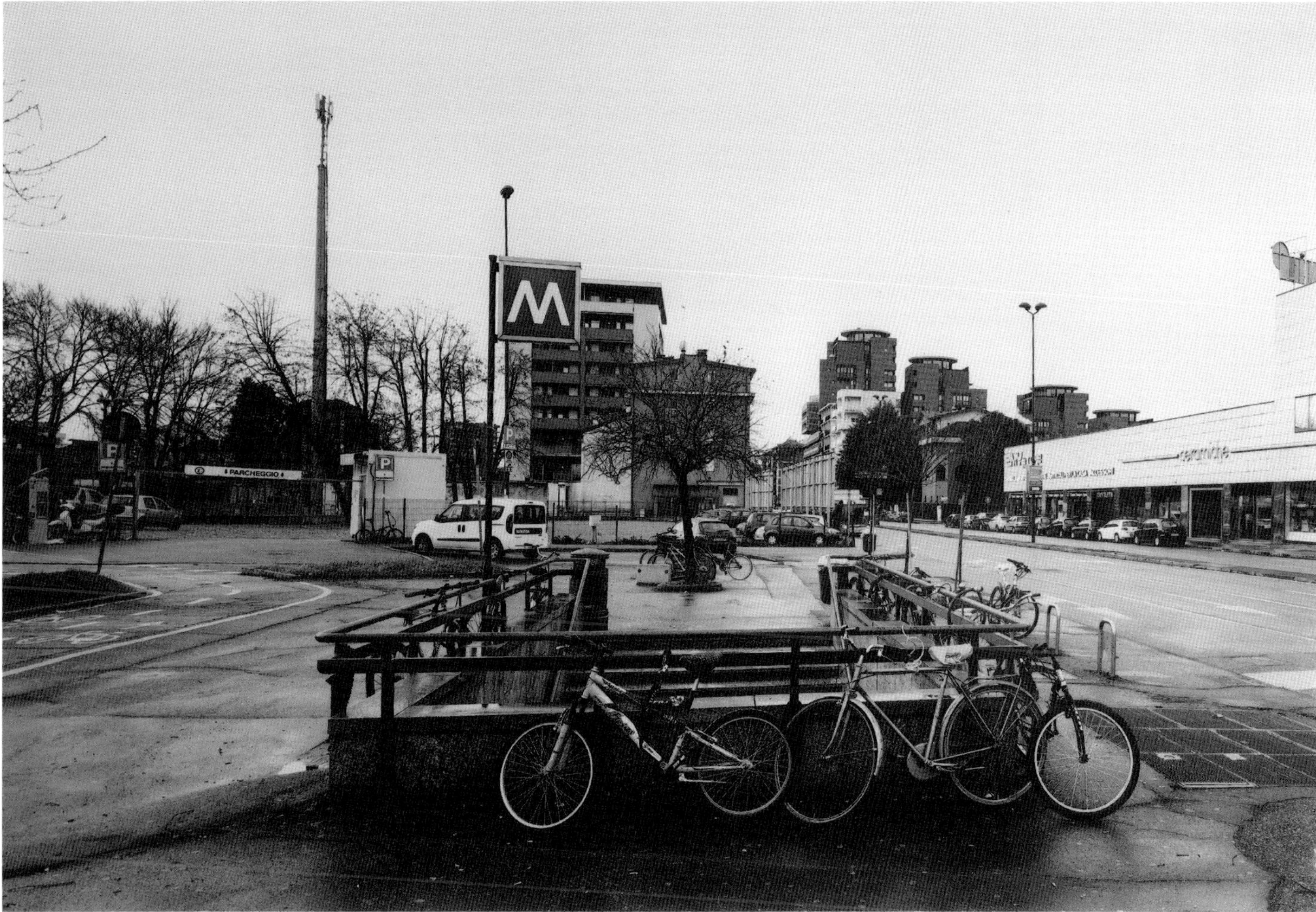
M
PARCHEGGIO

Bignami Parco Nord Station, M5 Line

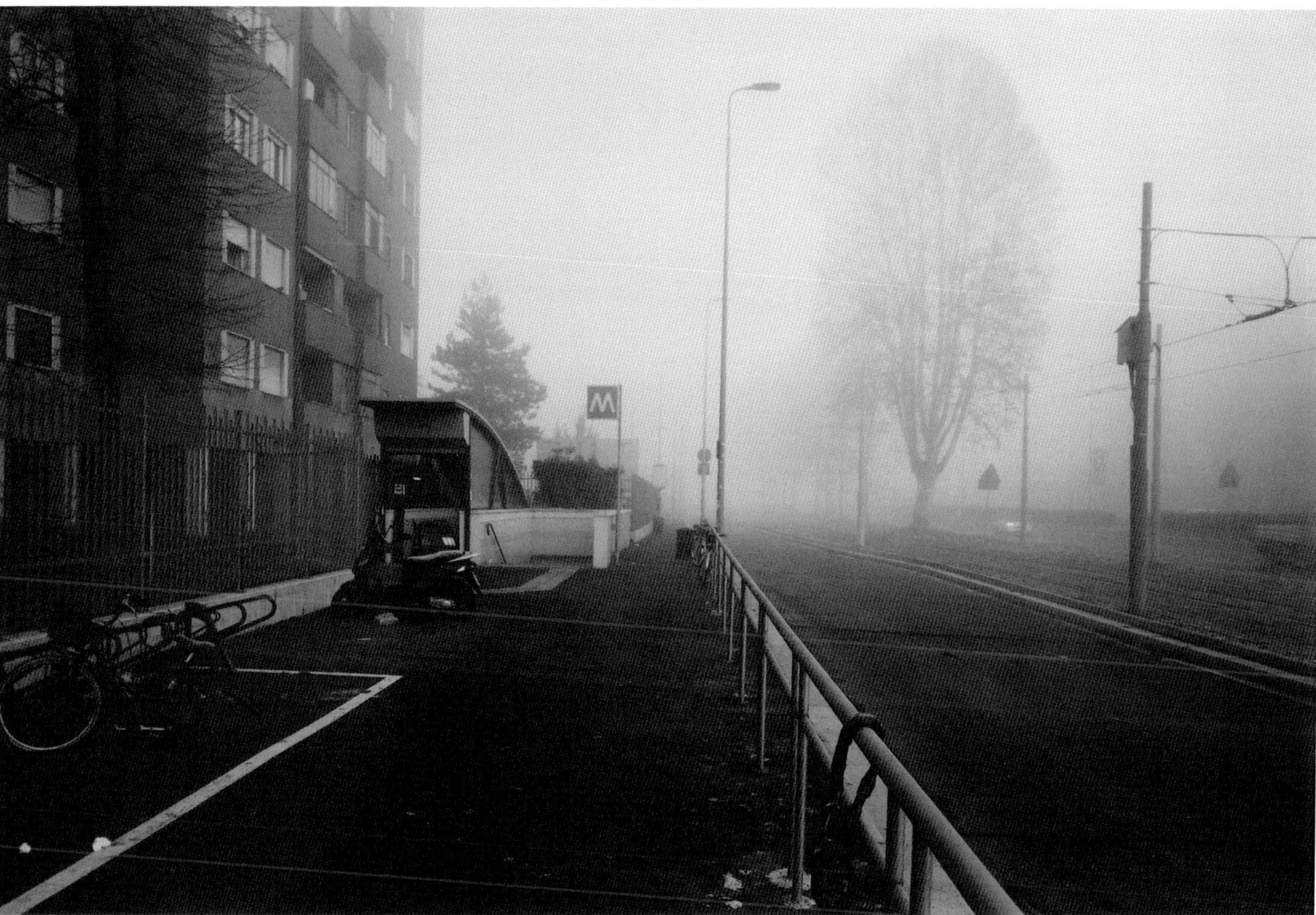
M

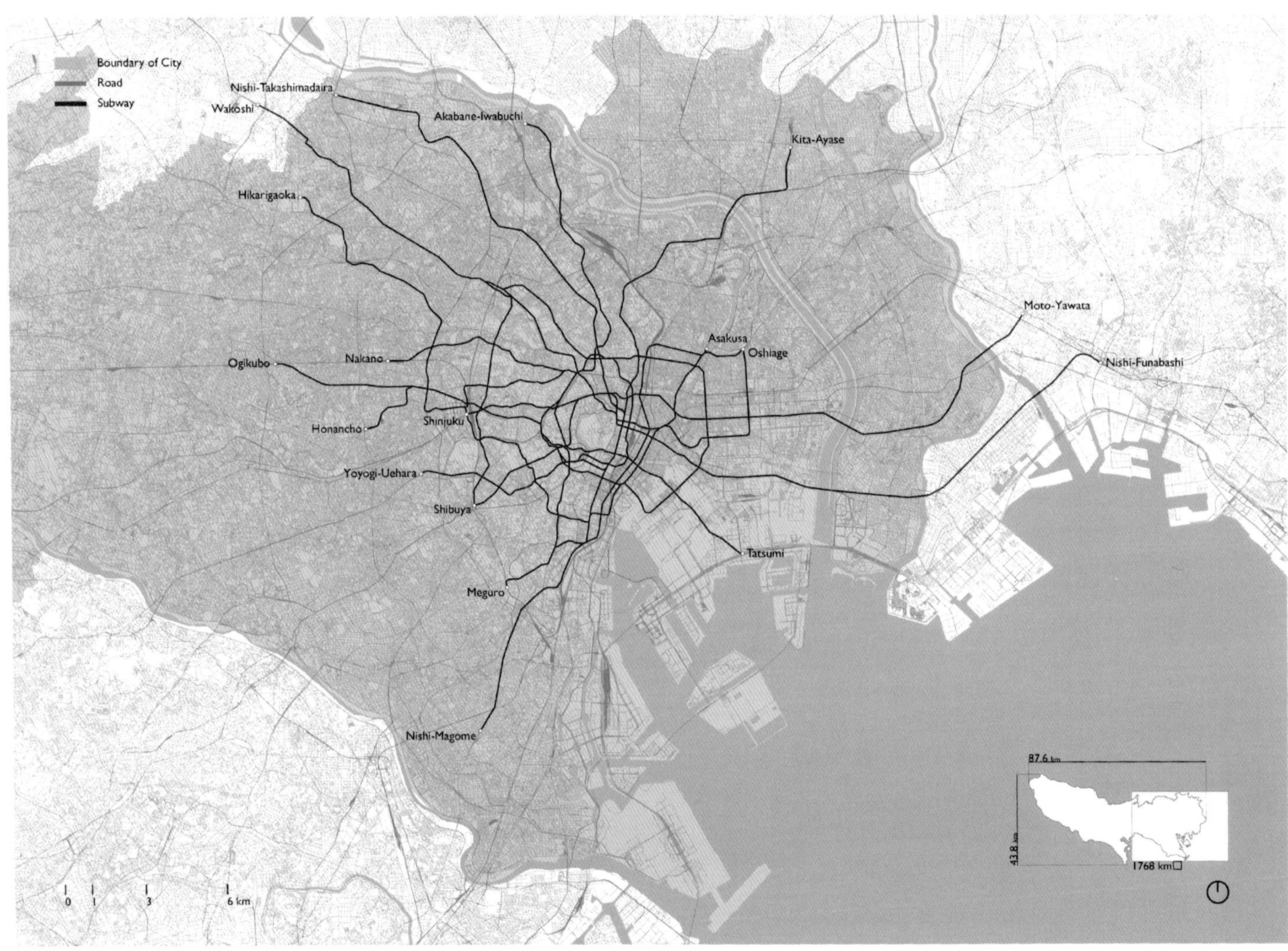

Boundary of City
Road
Subway
Nishi-Takashimadaira
Wakoshi
Akabane-Iwabuchi
Kita-Ayase
Hikarigaoka
Moto-Yawata
Asakusa
Oshiage
Nishi-Funabashi
Ogikubo
Nakano
Honancho
Shinjuku
Yoyogi-Uehara
Shibuya
Tatsumi
Meguro
Nishi-Magome
87.6 km
43.8 km
1768 km□
0
1
3
6 km

Tokyo Metro

Operated by Tokyo Metro Co. Ltd. and Toei Subway

Line network: 310 km
Annual ridership: 3,334 billion*

* http://www.railway-technology.com/, 2017

Terminal Stations (appearing in the photographic project):
- Asakusa, Ginza Line - Opened 1927
- Shinjuku, Shinjuku Line - Opened 1978
- Oshiage, Hanzomon Line - Opened 2003

In the following pages, the stations appear in counterclockwise order, starting from North.

70 Shinjuku Station, Shinjuku Line

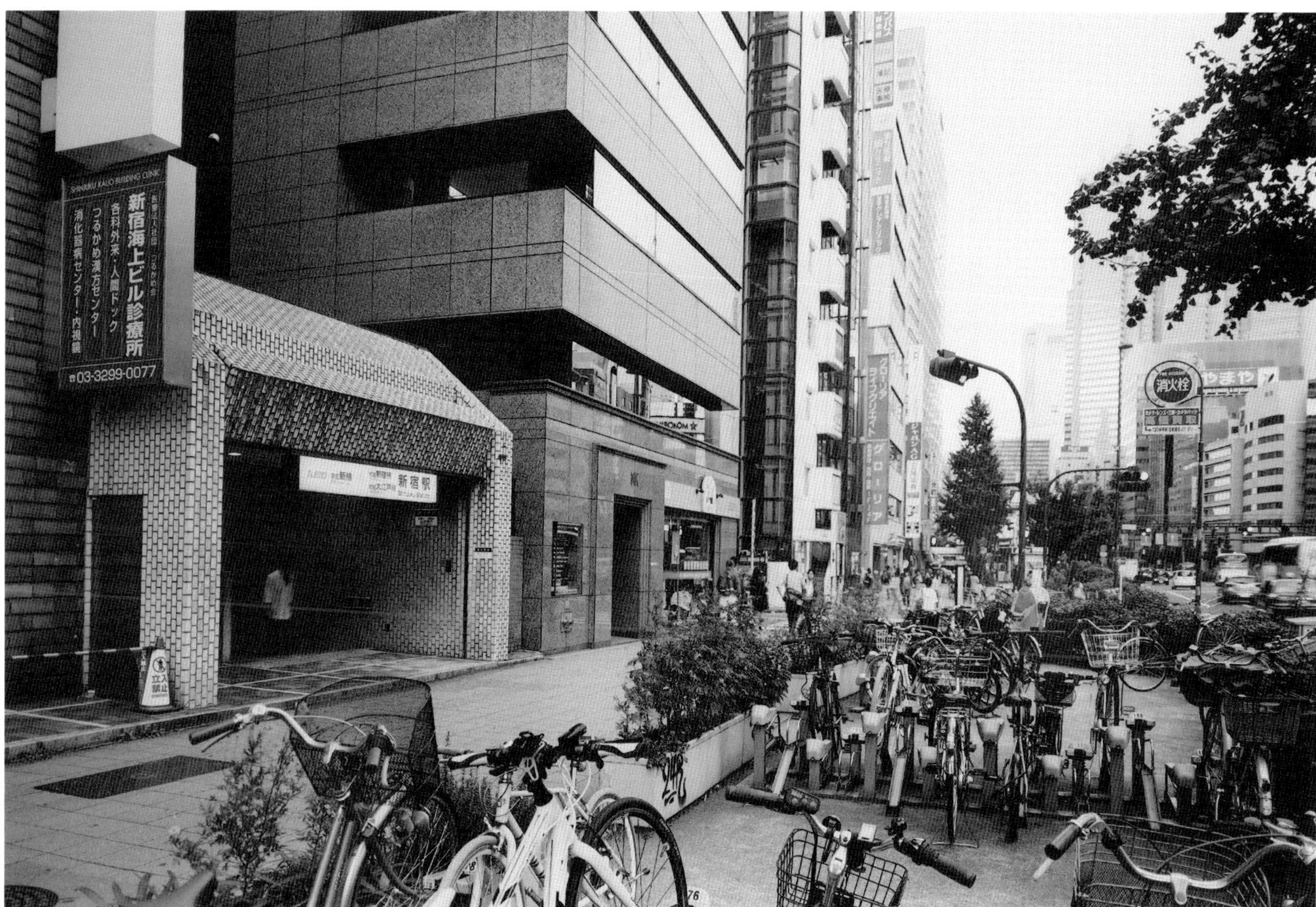
SHINJUKU KAIJO BUILDING CLINIC
新宿海上ビル診療所
各科外来・人間ドック
つるかめ漢方センター
消化器病センター・内視鏡
03-3299-0077
新宿駅
消火栓
やまや

72 Oshiage Station, Hanzomon Line

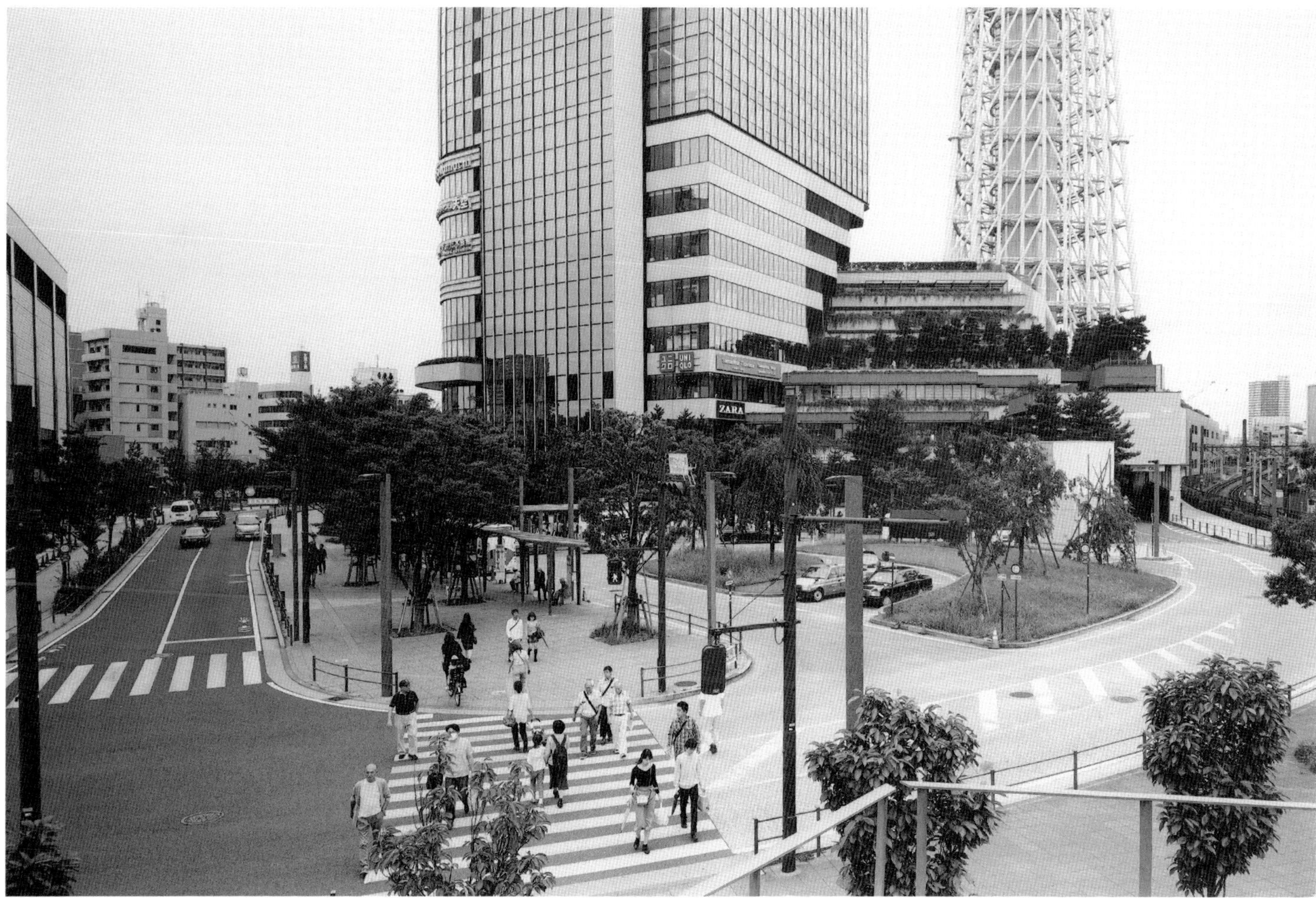
UNI
QLO
ZARA

74 Asakusa Station, Ginza Line

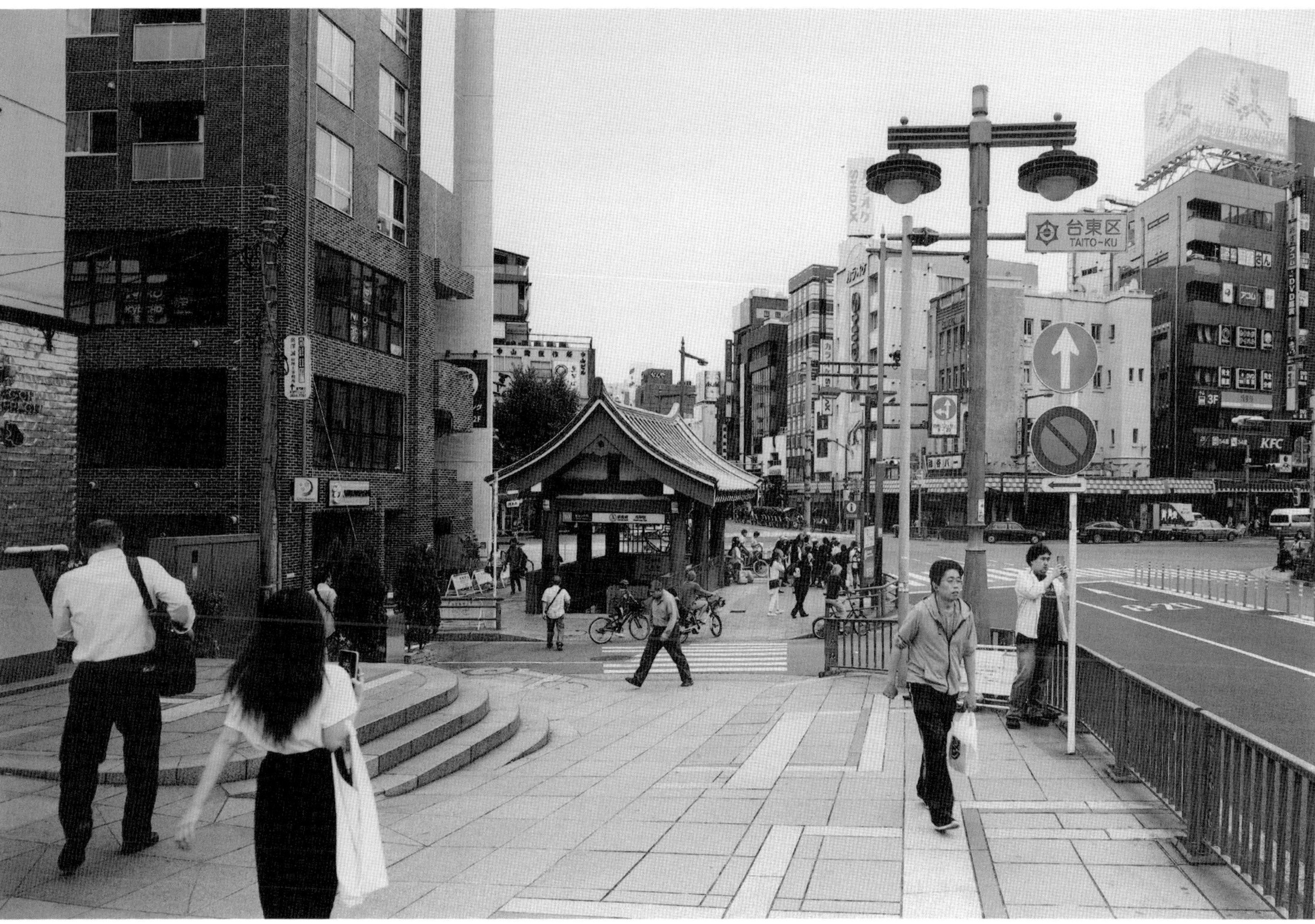
台東区
TAITO-KU
KFC

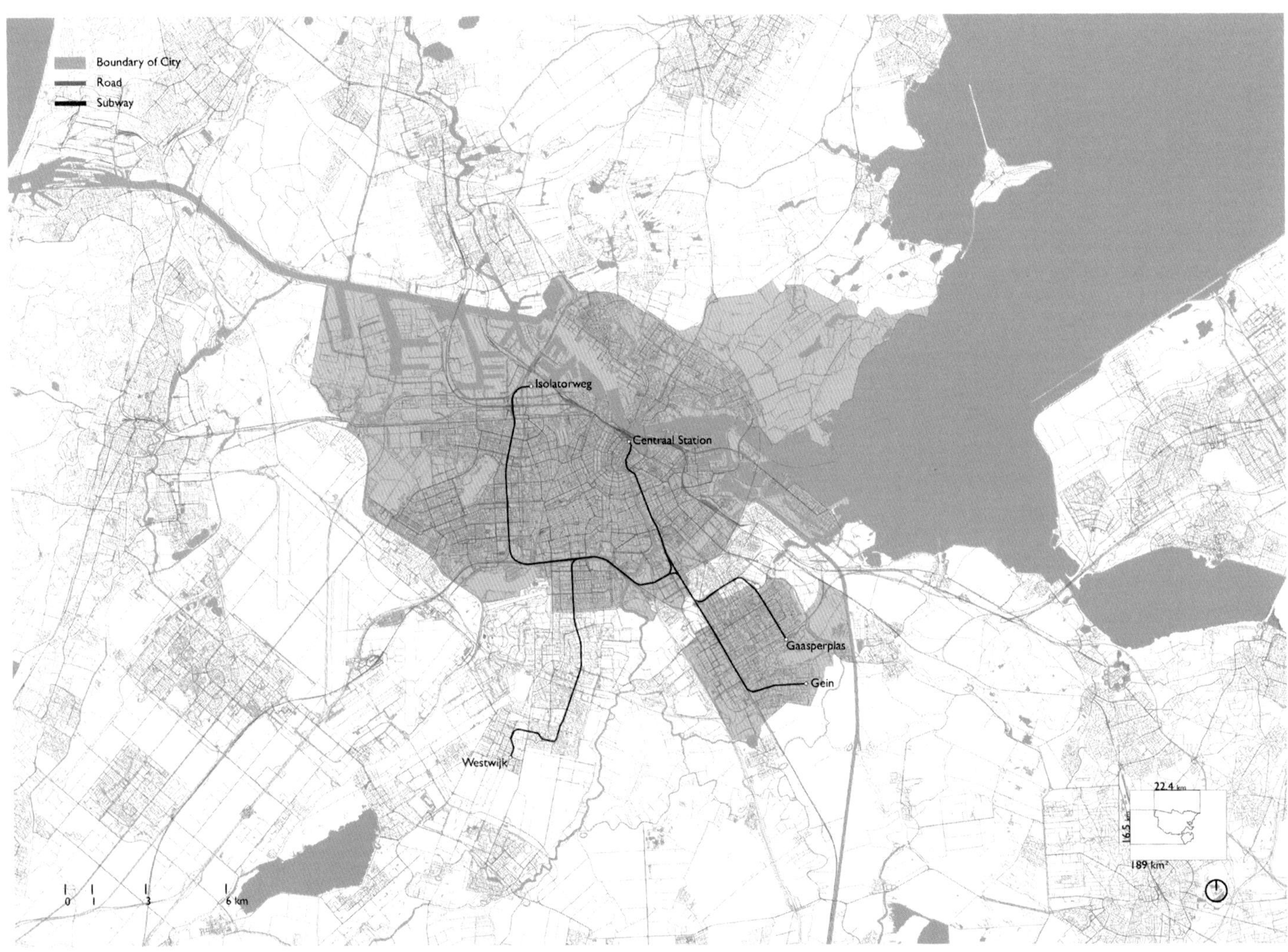
Boundary of City
Road
Subway
Isolatorweg
Centraal Station
Gaasperplas
Gein
Westwijk
22.4 km
16.5 km
189 km²
0
1
3
6 km

Amsterdam Metro

Operated by Gemeentelijk Vervoerbedrijf (GVB)

Line network: 31 km
Annual ridership: 71 million*

* Jaarverslag 2016, GVB Holding, 2017

Terminal Stations (appearing in the photographic project):
- Gein, Metro 50-54 Line - Opened 1982
- Westwijk, Metro 51 Line - Opened 2004

In the following pages, the stations appear in counterclockwise order, starting from North.

78 Westwijk Station, Metro 51 Line

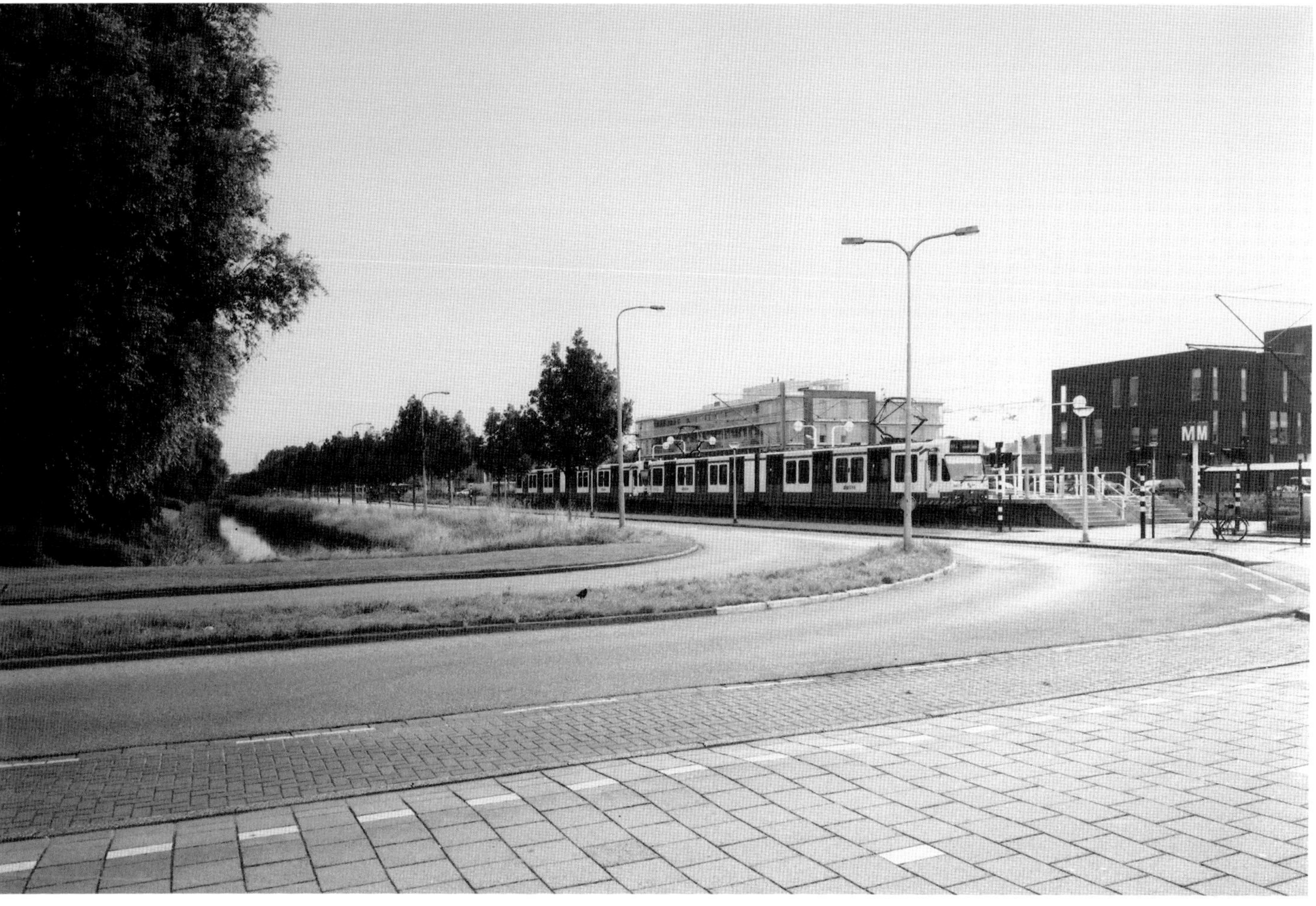
MM

80 Gein Station, Metro 50-54 Line

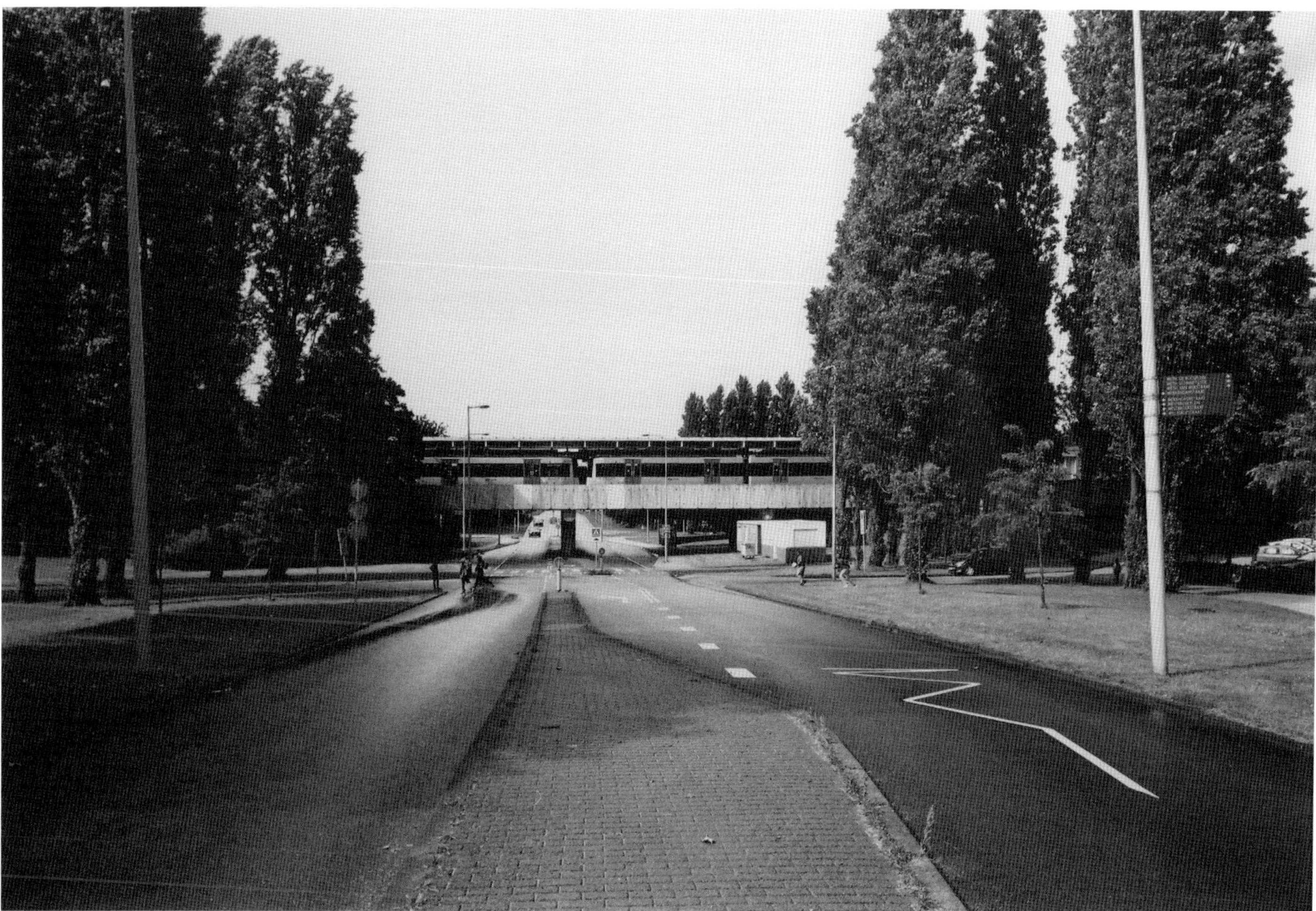

What can we see in The City at the End of the Underground?

A double account for to interpret a photographic project about the city today

by Alessandro Martinelli

Yes, it is. "The City at the End of the Underground" seems the title of a sci-fi novel that recounts a post-atomic world. Something *en-vogue*, today. Obviously, this is not the thing here, but this idea will help us situating and give meaning to the book, that presents the outcomes of a special photographic project.
If you scrolled through the pages, you have realized that this is the investigation of some Asian and Western cities at the terminal stations of their subway system -or underground, as they call it sometime. Anyway, while we keep in mind the post-atomic scenery, let's progress step by step, so as to avoid reaching too quickly the conclusions and deprive them of references.
The first thing that we have to do is ponder the relationships between photography and the contemporary city. Interestingly enough, these two have developed together. The historical series that represents the world largest city -a reliable indicator of the human urbanization and the scalar change of the urban phenomenon- changed inclination between the 18th and the 19th century.[1] During this particular time, the French Joseph Nicephore Niepce (1765-1833) took the first photography. That is, if projections were in use since the Renaissance, and some technologies to temporarily record them on planar media available since 1802, he finally achieved to long-lasting fix a projected image of reality. It was 1826. Against this new possibility of "freezing" life, the transformation of the city was quite the opposite. Indeed, it has "turned into a process."[2]

A refinement of Niepce's technology came to light when he teamed up with Louis-Jacques-Mandé Daguerre (1787-1851), a French dioramist. The innovation was a chemical one, i.e. depended on the substances used to imprint the image, but consisted on the definition of a proper camera obscura and opticals, too. As some argued, Daguerre played an important role because of his job.[3] That said, a digression about the diorama is probably necessary. This was an entertainment activity very popular at the beginning of the 19th century. It was sort of a movie theatre, where people can experience the transformation of large landscape images thanks to the control of lighting over and through their media: often, the mutation of diurnal into nocturnal views was at stake, an experience resembling the one offered today by the time-lapse. Now, it should be more clear the relation of Daguerre, photography, and the diorama. Anyway, what we must highlight is that this form of entertainment was not meant to reproduce reality, but providing some sensational experience. This had specific implications for the showcased images. Indeed, even if diorama claimed to reproduce reality -and it was partly doing it by introducing temporal aspects in the realm of the visual arts- the images were not *ex-found*, rather constructed for the sake of the aesthetic experience.
The very first camera obscura and its optical equivalent, i.e. the camera lucida, were born with similar purposes.[4] After the invention of the perspective during the Renaissance, these devices diffused to help the artists in crafting their drawings. To some extent, they were not props that simply aid reproducing reality, but devices that help to create the impression of a new "perspective style," often participating the reproduction of perspective scenes constructed according to the per-

ception made possible by the very same devices. That is, they were tools to build experiences, rather than copy reality. This is a subtle but crucial point, which draws on aesthetics reasons. Not by chance, the English painter Sir Joshua Reynolds (1723-1792) later stated that, thanks to such devices, "a painter would elaborate a representation of reality much better than the one offered by the devices only."[5]
So, in the beginning, photography was the reproduction of heavily constructed images, and it could not be different, due to the tradition of visual arts and the very long time of exposure that was required, among the other things.[6] Due to this, it was similar to the other visual arts. Probably, it was differing at the level of the aesthetic experience only, since, in the case of photography, this elaborated on the hyper-detailing of the image, something difficult to convey by other means.
A step further was the invention of the negative, by the British William Henry Fox Talbot (1800-1877), that opened the way for the mass reproduction of images, and the scaling down of both the media and the photographic device. More innovations came along this evolutionary line thanks to the flexible film in 1884, and the portable instantaneous camera in 1888 -i.e. the Kodak. Small and cheap, this was easy to use, too. As the advertisement recited: "You press the button, we do the rest."[7] Since then, the device has gone much further on. Indeed, beyond becoming integrated within our mobile phones, thus always on our side, it has finally become able to improve the quality of images by software processing.
As we can understand, the development of photography has been characterized by the progressive miniaturization, portability, instantaneity, facility, cheapness, and readiness of the device. It has been some sort of disruptive evolution.[8] This enabled the photography to enter the actual spaces and times of a city that, if no longer required some particular staging in order to be portrayed, has undergone much more than a simple growth.

Now, let us pass to this transformation and clarify how the city has "turned into a process," as previously mentioned.
Before the 18th century, all inhabited landscapes were quite stable phenomena. Their spatial transformation was very slow, and so it was the transformation of the socio-economic system. With little exchange between people, and economies greatly based on subsistence, the larger socio-economic systems were possible only after long times of development and consolidation. This allowed the spatial organization of inhabited landscapes to develop while mirroring the spatial organization of socio-economic systems. To some extent, the two were going hand in hand, consolidating each other, and the urban development often reflected the desire of turning the spatiality of socio-economic systems into an aesthetic experience. Not by chance, for long time the urban design participated the visual arts.
Then, with the advent of industrialization and infrastructure, the inhabited landscapes changed in two significant ways. First, people started to move in the larger cities while the infrastructure systems to stretch out and interweave. Second, the people entered the cities and a different socio-economic system, based on the production of surplus and the possibility of trade, rather than simple subsistence. This way, large-size cities have become the privileged form of inhabited landscape, but the urban space has also changed. Essentially, "the city as experience" entered a crisis.
Originally, the trade was not so important. It was too little, so the urban spaces did not really interact with it; rather, they mirrored the socio-economic relations and dignify them, if any design was applied. Then, after the socio-economic sys-

tem opened, trade has become necessary for to close all socio-economic relations. Due to this, it has become impossible for space to mirror these lasts. Indeed, they entered a state of constant transformation. To say it bluntly, before, any artisan knew in advance who he was producing for, then, the constant research for new customers has become a constituent part of any business, if not the major one. With trade becoming sort of connective tissue, space and the trade began dealing together to the solution of the socio-economic system. As a result, the geography of central places -i.e. the places to be- started to depend on the flow of people and -as we all know- the people call more people, but they also change their mind quite quickly. The spatial organization of cities can influence the flow, of course, but in ways that are not definitive, and the distribution of people has finally become variable, together with the central places and the requirements of accessibility.
So, the transformation of the inhabited landscapes corresponded to the movement of people to urban areas, their exponential growth, and the development of large infrastructure systems, but included the mutation of the city into a space that undergoes restless transformation. This has provided the basis for the crisis that we have mentioned. Indeed, how can we dignify a space, if the reasons of the operation can change faster than the time required to transform space?
The activity of urban design inevitably started changing, too. In this respect, the work of the Spanish Ildefonso Cerdà (1815-1876) is noteworthy. Acknowledging the transformations at stake, he defined a new set of priorities for urban design. The first concern became the redistribution of human flows by the means of the spatial organization of infrastructure, so as to avoid the concentration of locational advantages for trading in the hands of few. The second became the balance of the burden of maintenance provided by the growing infrastructure and the economies brought by the diffusion of locational advantages.[9] To grasp the novelty of the approach, we can ponder the almost coeval work of Camillo Sitte (1843-1903), known for his book "The City Planning According to Artistic Principles." The book had large diffusion, but developed as a reaction against the many contemporary urban designs based on hygienic norms and resulting in repetitive forms. In short, this was a simple plea against the loss of attention for the design of the city as experience.[10] Against this, Cerdà's work suggests that the happenings were not the effect of simple distraction.
Indeed, a full reconfiguration of the human system was at stake due to the rise of trade and infrastructure: a new society, a "new inhabitant," already entered the city and asked for spatial restructuring. This is because it depended on spatial devices -i.e. the infrastructure- both sophisticated and demanding in terms of maintenance. Without these, the "new inhabitant" could not simply exist but, since they started giving some hard constraints, they have also made the urban subject composed of human society and technology. To say it bluntly, with so much to pay for the management but so much need for infrastructure, has not this last entered some symbiotic relationship with us?[11] Not only, since the infrastructure both participates and weaves cities together, these have fused into continental megalopolises, and the idea of urban boundaries has been literally wiped out.[12]
In the light of this, the definition of a new spatial organization cannot do but precede the issue of the city as experience. Indeed, while the new urban subject began challenging the planners and designers, the city as experience had no other choice but to go back and question itself.

Unfortunately, in many ways, this question is still today ongoing.

To some extent, the crisis has paralleled with the issues brought by the development of photography to the representation of reality. After photography, this last has given up posing challenges that directly trigger an aesthetic concern: the effort of production has become so little that no concerns about the meaning of the operation arise. Other challenges may, but none directly linked to traditional aesthetics, rather to the authorization, policing, or the actuality of representation, e.g. those ones triggered by some curiosity for the unexpected, the forbidden, disappearing, the hidden, the aesthetic paradox, where photography stands as a proof of a unique reality. It is a different kind of aesthetic.[13] Because of this and the urban crisis, the happenings at the intersection of photography and the city are quite interesting.
In the beginning, following the pictorial tradition of the city, photography took charge of the panoramic view. Anyway, if there is a limited number of cities -London, Paris, and New York, i.e. the capitals of modernity- that attracted the photographic gaze in the 19th century, the viewpoint quickly diverged from these origins and diversified. First of all, it entered the street level against the aerial one, and it did not do it for practical reasons only. As early as Charles Negrè (1820-1880), the oddity of street figures and jobs became a photographic subject. Charles Marville (1816-1879) depicted the transformation of Paris from the ground level, too. This enabled him to venture the city and create an atlas of the disappearing urban atmosphere. Thomas Annan (1829-1887) documented the social condition, and he did it as sort of detective that enters those spaces where the middle-class would not go. Going on with the documentary gaze, Jacob Riis (1849-1914) investigated the overcrowded and infested tenements of the low-class. Then, Lewis Hine (1874-1940) recorded the urban transformations with a commitment to the relationship of men and the spatial context, e.g. the construction workers in the Empire State Building, or the immigrants in Ellis Island. Weegee (1899-1968) exploited a nocturnal and sensationalist point of view, often venturing the dangers or the violence of the city, and elaborating on the curiosity over moral extremes. Brassai (1899-1984) went further on and literally stalked the city at night, often peeping people in hotels, brothels, and nightclubs of the sort. Conversely, Eugene Atget (1857-1927) took pictures in the early morning, wandering before people could wake up and "showcasing sites, more than sights."[14] Indeed, he ventured into the spaces that, despite the absence of people, hold a strong sense of human presence. Of course, against this realist approach, other photographers portrayed people and spaces with modernist appearance, hinting a dynamic yet seemingly exceptional future, e.g. Jacques Henri Lartigue (1894-1986), or Ilse Bing (1899-1998).
Most interestingly, some others tried to portray the contemporary city as such, directly challenging the crisis at stake. Alfred Stieglitz (1864-1946) attempted to extract higher aesthetic experiences from the urban space, possibly suggesting the presence of some spiritualism embedded in the new city. First, he took minimal pictures at the street level, and then he started to picture the skyline from within the higher and higher floors of the buildings. The pictures became more and more somber, deprived of human figures, but finally "defeated by the city he sought to unify and idealize according to an underlying philosophy of meaning: [this city was] a condition based on disunity and fragmentation -some made world always hovering on the edge of mean-

inglessness."[15] From within this condition, Berenice Abbott (1898-1991) developed attention for those signs, letterings, and advertisements, that have progressively replaced the urban space in representing the city. Finally, Andres Kertesz (1894-1985) overcame the borders of everyday mental awareness. In his work, the city appears as a series of enigmas without meaning. Some talk of his viewpoint as the one of "tourist's exhilaration:"[16] while his pictures portray the unexpected -and most probably unnoticed- aesthetic occurrences of the city, such kind of "epiphanies" express simple observing, rather than knowing, and the amazement behind the search for a possible meaning. So, what happened? In short and quite roughly, we abandoned a pre-modern condition where the appearance of urban space was the outcome of an intentional aesthetic construction, and entered a condition where this intentionality is often lost. Anyway, something new has also emerged. Urban spaces passed from being an inanimate recipient of aesthetic will, to being -at least through the photographic gaze- an automatic producer of transitory aesthetic experiences, no matter if meaningless. Not only, this sort of paradox has become a resource. Indeed, photography has elaborated on the stupor behind the severed relation of experience and meaning. Actually, it has both exploited and contributed to the surprise. Indeed, those experiences framed by photography seem the result of unexpected, hidden, unknown, illegal, or unnatural forces. And the stupor in front of them can be so strong -when it comes to photography as a visual art- that gives momentum to such forces. As John Berger puts it, while trying to define what is art photography, "the degree to which I believe this [image] is worth looking at can be judged by all that [photography is] willingly not showing because it is contained within it. [..] Every photograph is in fact a means of testing, confirming, and constructing a total view of reality."[17] That is to say, in some strange ways, photography has contributed to the crisis of the city as experience, since it has mutated the perception of the issue in ambivalent form.

Considered this way the happenings of the late 19th and beginning of 20th century, let us now fast forward a century on and address the work of the Italian Gabriele Basilico (1944-2013). Indeed, his approach has greatly influenced the project shown by the book in your hands. He has provided a unique commentary on the city after the failure of post-war dreams in several European countries, especially Italy. In particular, he portrayed those structures, factories, and office buildings that express both the energies behind national redevelopment and those forces of conservative nature that changed the events into some tragic disappointment. Here it is the photographic gaze and the ambivalent perception of urban space! The subjects are usual buildings within their context, pieces from the background of everyday life. The pictures are taken in the early morning -the like of Atget- before that people can arrive and populate the spaces. The human presence is palpable, but everyone seems to have just left for some special reasons, probably. Yet, it is all normal. The result is, as Francesco Bonami puts it, "not a celebration of architecture and of its symbolic value but a discourse about the aesthetic value of architecture and the constant contradiction with its social function."[18]

Among the many projects by Basilico, one has stronger relevance here, i.e. "Sezioni del Paesaggio Italiano,"[19] developed for the Architecture Exhibition of La Biennale di Venezia 1996, in collaboration with the Italian architect Stefano Boeri. The project chronicles a trip through six "sections" of the Italian landscape, e.g. those linear areas that span between

Milan and Como, or Florence and Pistoia. Basilico wandered these corridors, each long about fifty kilometers, and turned his view away from the city centers for to study the happenings of the landscape. The objective was to contradict conventional perceptions and unveil those diffused urban agglomerations that span across kilometers of the landscape, with low density and quality of public space. Here, he portrayed with his distinctive style the building typologies that he encountered. If the project provided evidence to realize how the categories of city, suburban areas, and landscape were no more so clear with respect to urban design, architecture, and society, the outcomes of the work constitute a unique atlas of the individualistic ambitions of the Italians, projected on a multitude of buildings without civic context.
In the context of the happenings of city and photography, Basilico expresses an approach peculiar of the left-wing Italian intellectuals in the 70s. Among these, the aesthetic experience framed by the arts is often accompanied by social commentary. This implies the idea of "clinical" representation, where the aesthetic aspects give momentum to a social critique. Of course, we must remember that this cannot be misunderstood for the collection of scientific evidence. Rather, it is sort of an indirect political statement, where critique aligns with respect, as in the best realist tradition. This is what distinguishes Basilico from other photographers, that elaborated on aesthetic aspects only. Keep following Bonami, for Basilico, "photography is still a tool with which to document and represent society, to express 'truth;' the aesthetics were secondary."[20] In order to clarify it, we can compare him and the components of the Dusseldorf School of Photography.[21] Although Basilico shares with them from a methodological point of view, they exploit the contemporary city for to elaborate on the meaningless monumental occurrences that can be found within. But there is no critique, there. Not by chance, the images are often enlarged, and manipulated to amplify their effect. Basilico disagreed with all this. He considered himself an actual photographer, rather than artist, so he forced himself to remain faithful to his subjects and their *raison d'être* within the socio-economic context.

That said, we have reviewed more or less all the aspects necessary to outline the post-atomic world that we mentioned at the beginning. It is a world inhabited by human beings and infrastructure together. It is a world where the socio-economic system is wide open, always on the verge of disintegration. It is a world that, given the socio-technical and open character, is covered by infrastructure, "engulfed" by never-ending cities. Unfortunately, these last do not necessarily look nice, either provided with good urban space. Often, they do not embody a human aesthetic will. Rather, they have a rhapsodic aesthetic capability, unfortunately distanced from the production of meaning. Not only, this is a world where the visual arts elaborates on the divergence of aesthetics and meaning. Sometime it is the possibility to venture new experiences, sometime it is the possibility of a political critique. Isn't this quite post-atomic? It is like a dystopian sci-fi movie, almost absurd, even if it seems normal when we look outside the window.[22]
Anyway, the point is that this is the operative context of the photographic project here at stake. There is the infrastructure, the boundaries of the city, the quality and meaning of urban space, photography as art, and an ambivalent interrogative about the urban condition. Due to this, the work shares with Basilico's one. It just moves a bit further on in the realm of the "clinical" methodology. The reasons are not to be found in the attempt to draw an

impartial judgment. Rather, they are in the attempt to cope with one more aspect of our world, i.e. globalization, that puts additional distance between aesthetics and meaning. Today, anybody can end up living in disparate areas of the planet, inhabiting spaces that are culturally alien from his birthplace, despite any resemblance.
Originated from within this condition, the project elaborates a commentary on the city while tries to make sense of this global ambiguity, a challenge that requires a bit more of scientific approach in order not to get lost.
Methodologically speaking, science essentially means a set of strict constraints to a repetitive work over diverse subjects. So, first of all, there is the choice for pondered comparison between cities of diverse continental areas. Then, there is the choice for a precise spatial occurrence -i.e. the city at the terminal station of the subway- and consistency of the work. Finally, if all pictures are black and white and taken in the early morning, the viewpoint portrays the city while provides some understanding of the pedestrian space around the subway station. All this does not mean that the investigation has been driven by an "automatic pilot." Rather, it means that this was developed while keeping meaningful connections with crucial aspects of our world. It also means that, thanks to the clear definition of the operative context provided by these constraints, the work of the photographer has been liberated, rather than enchained by a frustrating attempt to develop some prior knowledge of the scenes portrayed.
Actually, there is another aspect hidden in this "clinical" approach, but this does not draw on science. The work follows Basilico's methodology but chooses the urban space as subject, rather than any urban architecture. The effect is particular: the series starts to revolve around a reference point, the essence of which roots in the relation between man, the world, and the shape of the city. Finally, the most interesting aspect of this work is that makes us pondering about this reference point while we consider the possible ambivalence between science and urban space. In some ways, this reveals how, within the post-atomic scenery that we have depicted, the urban space can be a device to know and interpret the world.
In the end, the author of the photography is not a professional of planning or design. He is just a global citizen that, like many others, has been visiting and living in many places, and has used the urban space in order to understand and develop an opinion over the world. Due to this, the photography project is a commentary on the city as well as on the way we live after urbanization and globalization. Does not have an existential vibe the choice for the outpost of mass transit as a reference point at the border between the known and unknown?
All this makes the project very different from others of similar kind, e.g. the "Report from the edge" recently developed by the Urban report group.[23] This last investigated a series of episodes embodying the developmental narratives taken by four European cities at their edges. Each episode was defined after desk research and a series of meetings with the stakeholders. As a result, when we look at the outcomes, we can see a partial perspective on the cities represented, that requires an extensive description in order to be really understood. Indeed, "Report from the edge" aims to offer a visual reference for the decision makers with respect to some developmental episodes where intentionality is questioned. It is a reportage developed for professionals by professionals that are interested in specific landscapes under transformation. In short, it is not an existential quest. It does not tell us how the urban space as such can offer a perspective on the global

world. It does not tell us how we could find meaning for the urban space after a long and dark period -a metaphorical underground- during which we used to speak about the city as "junkspace,"[24] a scrap yard where the things get lost and accumulate.

With this in mind, we can finally venture into the photographic outcomes of the project here at stake. Basically, they portray all the terminals of Taipei and Milano subway. Images of Tokyo and Amsterdam can be found as well, and they offer comparative ground to test the impressions emerging out of the first two cities. More materials can be finally found in the appendix, and they include secondary images from other kinds of cities.
Besides personal reasons, Taipei and Milano were chosen for the comparable size, surface area, and governance system. Amsterdam was chosen since it is the main city of the Netherlands, that have comparable size and surface area with the island of Taiwan. Finally, Tokyo was chosen since it is the main city of Japan, the planning culture of which had strong influence on Taiwan, due to the Japanese occupation between 1895 and 1945 and the following cultural ties.
At the very first sight, the series seem the portrait of one single city. This asks for our eyes to get accustomed before to suggest something out of the comparison between different cities. Then, we see it. In Milano, the public space at the exit of the subway stations is greatly deprived of public green, furniture, and a qualified paving. It seems that, outside the well know historical center, there is no public space. The density is lower and the environment has seldom the characters of the street, rather of the road. Sometimes, we see large and silent buildings occupying the image, and the open space is most often surrounded by various kinds of fences: concrete, metal mesh, iron bars, hedges, etc... An atmosphere of desolation and abandonment can be perceived. In Taipei, we witness a different condition. There is high density, the buildings are not silent, there is some life behind the walls. The paving is qualified; car space is not necessarily ordered but marked by many signs that regulate the traffic. We do not see any fence, and the green turns from hedges into one component of the public space. Actually, it does not look any different from the city center.
To some extent, the images of Tokyo and Amsterdam follow this dichotomy, even if in a different form. More precisely, in Tokyo, there is such an urban density and quality of public space, that no marginality can be perceived, at least in the eyes of someone that is not Japanese. In Amsterdam, there is qualified paving, but the city seems to leave space for nature, sparsely occupied by good-looking but isolated infrastructure and built structures. In short, the human presence seems to fade away in the loneliness.
In the light of this, a double realization comes to us. First, against the diffused narrative that speaks about the inescapability of the urban experience, somewhere the city seems to finish. That is, the urban dynamics do not finish -the presence of infrastructure clarifies this- but the urban space gives place to something else. Then, against the political-cultural narratives of European planning and design, often characterized by the "value" of the public space, the margins of the European city have less quality and intensity than the Far Eastern ones.
Here, given that this is not an academic research, we can only make an educated guess about the reasons behind such happenings. Probably, the Far Eastern habit of transit-oriented development is part of the answer, given that this often associates mass transit and mixed-use development without the "ideological burden" of the historical city center. An-

other aspect is perhaps a reduced space for urbanization, but the outcome is that the urban development in the Far East seems greatly based on spatial principles. Probably, another side of the answer is the European habit to elaborate on the historical association of city center and commercial development, where mass transit comes at the service of the last rather than urban development. The narrative of the car, together with the one of individual freedom and leisure, could have contributed, too.

Anyway, against these findings, the viewpoint of the photographic project, that uses the urban space as a device to interpret the world, suggests that some clear narrative of development should be defined for the urban boundaries. But this cannot be a simple abandonment of the urban space and living intensity, that gives space to nothing or nature but not the landscape. The pictures reveal the desolation emerging out of this. Neither this narrative can be a simple repetition of the urban center. Indeed, this would not contribute to a long-term characterization and qualification of the city. To some extent, nor Europe, either the Far East satisfies us, but we already know that, when we go to the margin of the city, we wish to see something different. A narrative that is local but bigger than the urban one. Maybe, this is the landscape as such, maybe something else, but we should find a way to bring it into the frame of the experience where the city ends, the frame to which "The City at the End of the Underground" entrusted itself.

1. See Chandler,T. (1987). Four Thousand Years of Urban Growth: An Historical Census. The Edwin Mellen Press. And Modelski, G. (2003). World Cities: –3000 to 2000. Faros 2000. And Morris, I. (2013). The Measure of Civilization. Princeton University Press.

2. See Cavalletti, A. (2005). La città biopolitica: mitologie della sicurezza (The biopolitical city: mythologies of security). Bruno Mondadori. Elaborating on the perspective of French philosopher Michel Foucault (1926-1984) with respect to the rise of biopolitics, i.e. the extension of governance powers over the production and reproduction of life itself, the book reviews the development of modern security paradigms in the urban space. In this context, the definition of the "city turning into a process" comes to highlight a radical transformation within the relationship of society, the organization of inhabited space, and the governance.

3. See Gernsheim, H. and A. (1968). L. J. M. Daguerre: The History of the Diorama and the Daguerreotype. Dover Publications. The book reviews the relation of Daguerre and Niepce, as well as the private and public appropriation of Niepce's invention by Daguerre's activity. Indeed, the improvement of photography achieved by the last profited from his public persona, and the way he handled publicity in relation to the French Academy of Science and Government, that later supported the diffusion of photography as a French trademark.

4. The theory of photography has been available for some time before photography. Indeed, according to the chronicles, this was already outlined by Leonardo da Vinci, although the first published account is "Magia Naturalis" by Giovanni Battista della Porta, published in 1558. This theory brought two devices, i.e. the camera obscura, and later the camera lucida. The first -of the same kind as in photography later on- derived from what was first used by Arab astronomers in the tenth century to observe the sun without looking directly at it, and offered an inverted image of reality that could be traced by the artist. The second offered an optical superimposition of the subject being viewed and the surface upon which the artist is drawing, as in a photographic double exposure. This allowed the artist to duplicate key points of the scene on the drawing surface.

5. See Reynolds, J. (1891). Discourses. McClurg and Company. This is the proceedings of a series of lectures delivered at the British Royal Academy of Arts between 1769 and 1790. Interestingly enough, at the Science Museum of London, there is a camera obscura once owned by Sir Joshua Reynolds. It is a miniaturized model that was made to be the size, shape, and appearance of a large book when collapsed. Supposedly, it really prefigured the portability of the camera.

6. Noteworthy, Daguerre's early image was the "Interieur d'un Cabinet Curiositè" (1837), a wunderkammer, sort of an encyclopedic collection of objects regarded as a microcosm or theater of the world, a memory theater. This is to say it was a heavily constructed scene, and deprived of any text, since Daguerre's early photographic system produced mirrored images, the reality of which could be invalidated by any reversed texts.

7. George Eastman patented the flexible film and then developed an appropriate camera. First it was the Detective, and then the Kodak together with the slogan "You Press the Button, We Do the Rest." Part of his well-known success came because from his business sense, that allowed him to see the potential in photography for amateurs. He believed this could attract two kinds of people. The first was the true amateur, who was willing and able to devote time and

money. He had interests in all aspects. The second simply wanted pictures as mementos of daily life but was hardly interested in learning how to do the rest. Eastman believed this second kind was large in number, so set about separating picture taking and processing. Customers had to simply take their pictures and send the camera to the Kodak factory. There, the film was separated from the camera, developed, and then prints were made from each negative and returned to customers, along with the negatives, the camera, and a new roll of film. Thanks to the "We Do the Rest" campaign and business model, the Kodak became wildly popular and dominate business competition for years.

8. See Christensen, C. (1997). The Innovator's Dilemma. Harvard Business Review Press, The book drafts the idea of disruptive innovation. Considering evolution the results of a series of innovation of certain kind over a specific system, disruptive evolution can be considered the effect of a series of disruptive innovations. This last is a definition originated in business theory, that stands for the innovations creating new markets and value networks, eventually disrupting the existing ones, and displacing established market-leading firms, products, and alliances. Photography kept evolving enlarging the diffusion of the system, but also the reach and capability. Not only, it also integrated with other aspects of our life, along with the line of what we presented as disruptive evolution.

9. See Arturo Soria y Puig (1999). Cerdá: the five bases of the general theory of urbanization. Electa. And Martinelli, A. (2014). Urban metabolism and urban design. Phd dissertation, Mendrisio. Cerdà was originally trained as an engineer at the first Spanish engineering school in Madrid. He joined the civil service and lived in various cities before settling in Barcelona, where he became interested in politics and the study of urban planning. When the local government gave in to public pressure and allowed Barcelona's city walls to be torn down, he realized the need for a city expansion that would be feasible to be realized, sustainable to be managed, and of course livable, unlike the congested, epidemic-prone old town within the walls. When he failed to find a suitable reference, he undertook the task of writing one from scratch while designing the extension, borrowing technological ideas that were disparately adopted for to create a modern integrated urban design theory and urban design for the city of Barcelona. His theoretical opus magnum is the "General Theory of Urbanization," published in 1856, but represents only a part of a larger unfinished production, that must be understood as a unitary theoretical corpus addressing the modern urban condition in integrated form. If his work is often ascribed to the list of hygienist urban designers, his approach is actually more complex and attempts to acknowledge and provide an answer to the modern transformation of the urban subject.

10. See Collins, G.R. and C. (1965). Camillo Sitte and the Birth of Modern City Planning. Random House. And Bohl, C., and Lejeune, J-F. (2009). Sitte, Hegemann and the Metropolis. Routledge. Sitte was art historian and architect, that traveled around Europe to identify spatial aspects contributing to the quality of urban space, and received a lot of attention in 1889 with the publication of his "City Planning According to Artistic Principles," then re-edited five times before 1922, and translated in several languages. The book put forward the idea that the "urban room," i.e. a defined urban space around the experiencing man, should be the leading motif of urban design, turning away from the pragmatic, hygienic planning procedures that were diffusing at the time. Mainly an urban planning theory book, it had a deep influence in architecture, as the two disciplines were strongly considered intertwined by Sitte. According to him, the most important task of the designer was not to define the architectural shape of a building, but the contribution to the urban space. In this respect, must be mentioned how he based his analysis on aesthetics evaluation, not concerned with those historical circumstances that generated the urban forms. While he feared that urban design could become a technical task, all of this brought him to intentionally disregard the transformation of the urban subject, this way showcasing in an indirect form the crisis of the "city as experience."

11. See Graham, S., and Marvin, S. (2001). Splintering Urbanism: networked infrastructure, technological mobilities, and the urban condition. Routledge, and Swyngedouw, E. (2009). The city as hybrid: On nature, society and cyborg urbanization in Capitalism, Nature, Socialism Journal. Thanks to the work of several scholars of political economy, during the 2000s and 2010s the notion of the city as a socio-technical system -or the cyborg as the urban subject- has been developed for to extend the reach of social criticism outside the purely social realm. This was done in the light of realizing how the interaction with infrastructure and technological implementations could embed social inequalities in the inhabited space. While the conceptual framework draws on the notion of cyborg, i.e. an organism with organic and technological parts, this also helped in understanding the complex interaction between society and nature, that is articulated through the infrastructure and can both constraint society and create a structurally unsustainable use of natural resources.

12. See Gottmann, J. (1961). Megalopolis. The Urbanized Northeastern seaboard of the United States. The Twentieth Century Fund. The book is the first to conclude that modern region's cities, while discrete and independent, can become uniquely tied to each other through the intermeshing of their suburban zones, taking on some characteristics of a single, massive city. See also, Lefebvre, H. (1970). La révolution urbaine (The urban revolution). Gallimard. Here, it is advanced the thesis that, at the mid of last century, the world population is already fully urbanized in terms of way of life, due to the advent of the modern socio-economical condition.

13. See Clarke, G. (1997). The Photograph. Oxford University Press. The book, used as the main reference for the following review of photography, presents an account of the photograph's historical development and elucidates the insights of major thinkers on the subject, e.g. Roland Barthes and Susan Sontag. In particular, the book provides an examination of photography's main subject areas –i.e. landscape, the city, the portrait, the body, and reportage- and some detailed analysis of

exemplary images in terms of cultural and ideological contexts. By the means of this, the book highlights the major aesthetic themes and approaches to photography as visual art. See also Berger, J. (1972). Understanding a Photograph. In Berger, J. (1975) Selected Essays and Articles: The Look of Things, Viking. In Berger's work, there are ideas drawing from Walter Benjamin's approach to the art and mechanical reproduction, but he further elaborates on how photography contributed that some fidelity to the subject of representation has given way to the interests of the viewers.

14. See Clarke, G. (1997). Idem. pp. 89-91

15. See Clarke, G. (1990). The City as Ideal Text: Manhattan and the Photography of Alfred Stieglitz, 1890-1940. In Mulvey, C., and Simons, J. (1990). New York City as Text, Palgrave Macmillan, pp. 12-27.

16. See Clarke, G. (1997). Idem. pp. 92-97.

17. See Berger, J. (1972). Idem. p. 3

18. See Bonami, F. (2001). Gabriele Basilico 55. Phaidon. p. 17

19. Besides the exhibition, the project is showcased in Basilico, G., and Boeri, S., (1997) Sezioni del paesaggio italiano, Art&. It is useful to quote the frontispiece: "this research studies the disordered and significant changes that have taken place in recent years in the Italian landscape. It is not so much the great buildings, the neighborhoods or the new infrastructures that have changed the face of our territory: it is rather a multitude of solitary and crowded buildings, like houses, sheds, shopping centers, buildings, garages, workshops. They are small buildings, often leaning against each other in an incongruous way, scattered in the landscape in a decomposed way, expressing small fragments of our society and our economy: the family, the small business, the distribution, the store, the club, the storage area. A dust of artifacts that, reflecting the state of our costume and our way of producing, have grown in the indifference of politics and cultured architecture, literally coming to disrupt the appearance and nature of the Italian territory, from north to south and in every region."

20. See Bonami, F. (2001). Idem. p. 18

21. See Gronert, S. (2010). The Dusseldorf School of Photography. Aperture. The Dusseldorf School is a group of artists, including Andreas Gursky, Candida Höfer, Thomas Struth, Axel Hütte, and Thomas Ruff, who studied under Bernd and Hilla Becher at the Kunstakademie Düsseldorf in the 1970s and rose to prominence in the 1980s. These artists' works are characterized by a sober, documentary quality, "straight-on topographic" views of landscapes, a major focus on cityscapes or interior environments, and the minimization of the human figure. Aided by new technical capabilities in digital photography and printing, a hallmark of the group has been a combination of dizzying detail and monumental size, giving the works an immersive quality and contributing to a blurring the boundaries of photography and painting.

22. In reality, there is much more that adds to this post-atomic scenario, let us just think about the influences of the Internet, social media, and the paraphernalia of personal technologies that we use every day, but this is out of the scope of work and discussion here.

23. Developed in four European cities between 2016 and 2016 by Urban reports, a European network of documentary photographers working on architecture and landscape by developing reportages at the territorial scale, the project "Report from the edge of the city" explores urban changes by investigating the geographic boundaries. The project uses documentary photography as a reading tool for contemporary territorial identity and a visual evidence of how the habits, society, and economy may influence and affect the urban margins. In this perspective, the photographic reading becomes some rough material for producing ideas and inspirations that can be integrated into the processes of planning and policy-making. The focus on the city boundaries derives from these being today at the center of the metropolitan strategic visions and long-term transformation plans. The four cities were Madrid, Rotterdam, Turin, and Milan. In Madrid, the project focused the huge urban transformations altering the fragile relationship of the city and countryside. In Rotterdam, the project investigated the administrative limits of the city, where the monofunctional areas dominate. In Turin, the documentary catches the urban transition of the borders, where the industrial heritage is the main feature. In Milan, the project portrayed how highways and transport hubs define the city.

24. See Koolhaas, R. (1995). Junkspace. In Koolhaas, R. (1995). S, M, L, XL. The Monacelli Press. The text, where the word junkspace is presented for the first time, elaborates in seminal ways on the idea that the city has been substituted by a highly commercialized environment that lacks any real value or meaning.

The City at the End of the Underground

addenda

In the following section, a series of additional pictures from Dubai, Berlin, and Kaohsiung can be found. These are materials from the photographic studies and drills that were implemented during the development of the project.

Dubai
>
Creek Station
Green Line

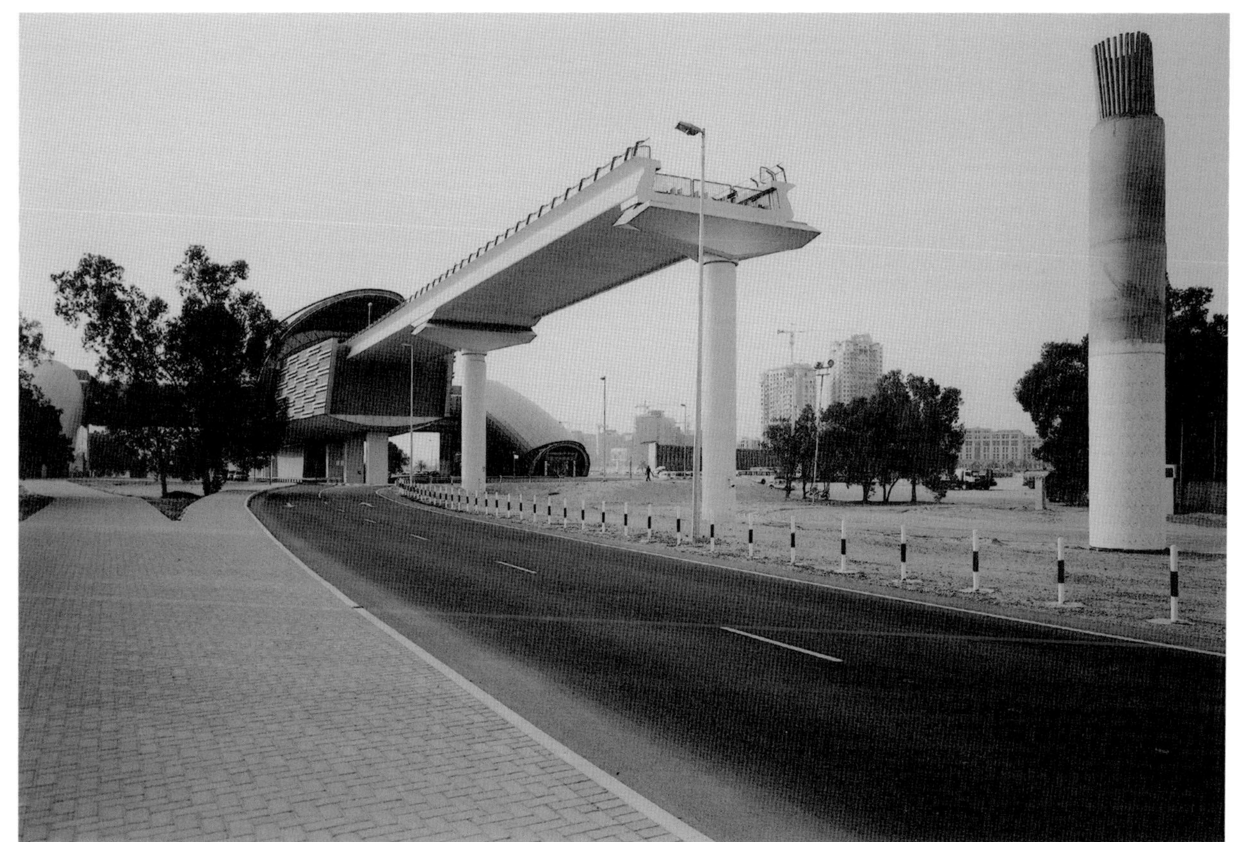

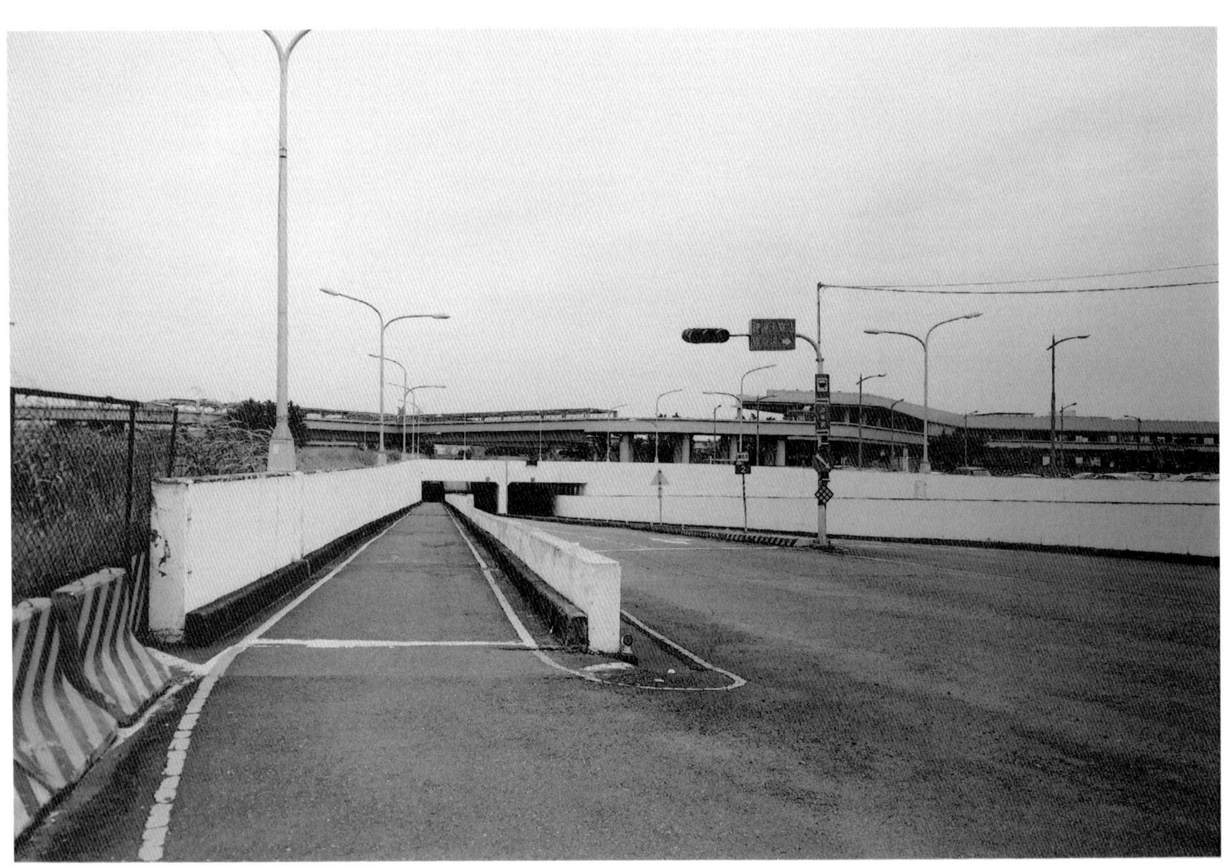

Daliao Station
Orange Line

Kaohsiung
< >
Sizihwan Station
Orange Line

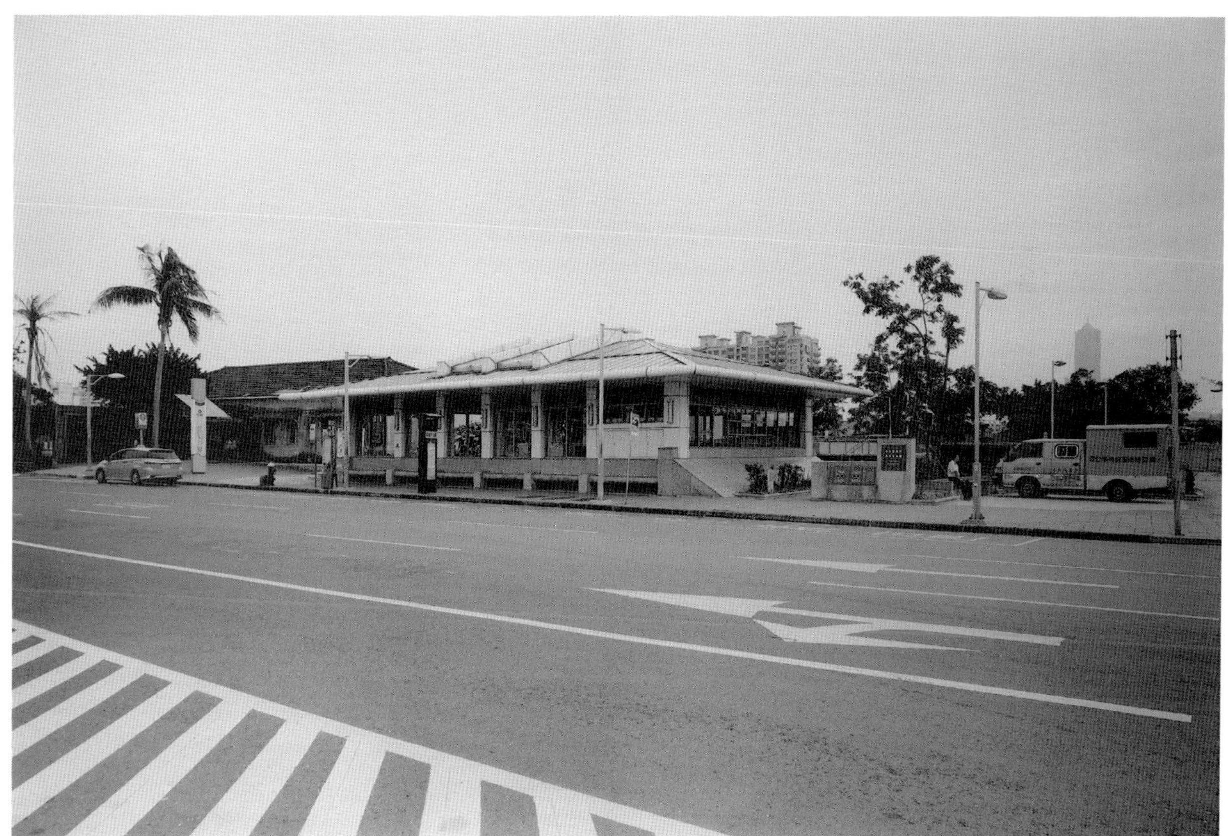

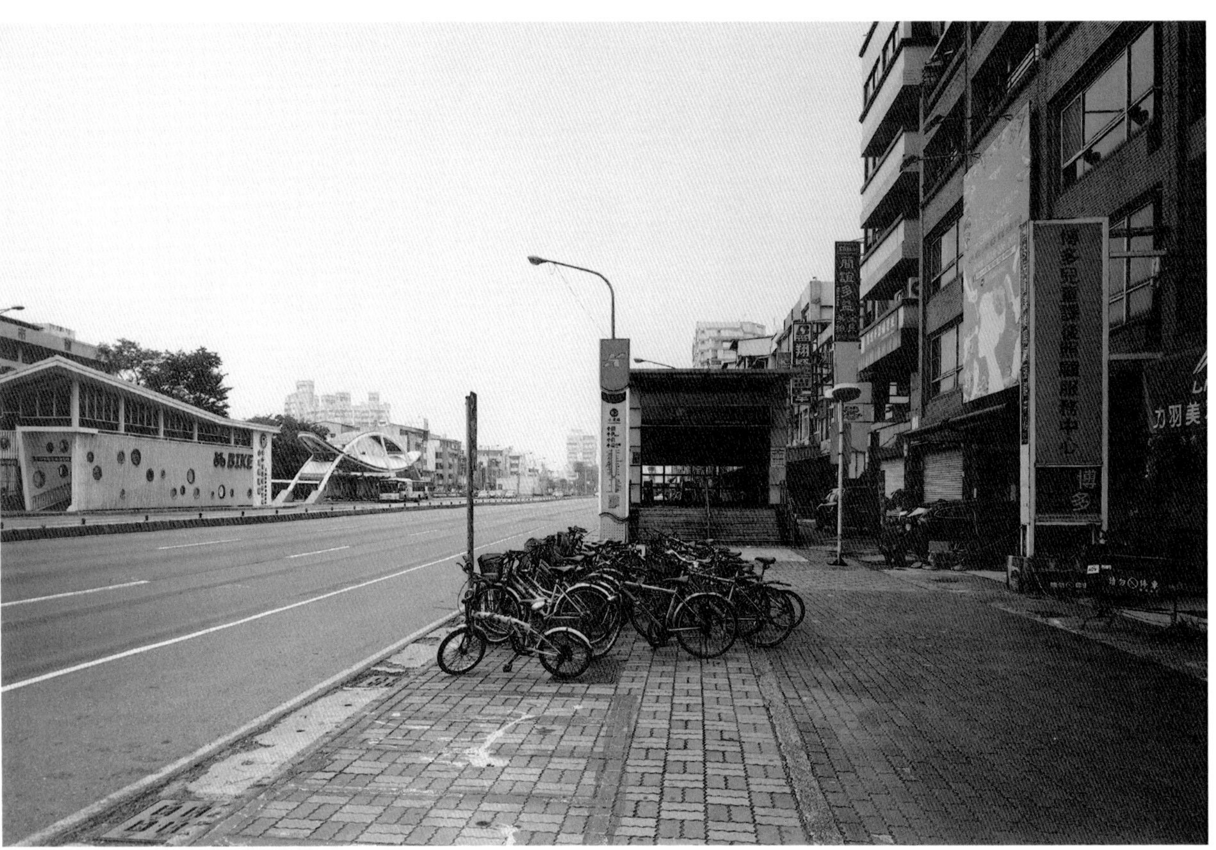

Siaogang Station,
Red Line

Kaohsiung
< >
Gangshan South
Station, Red Line

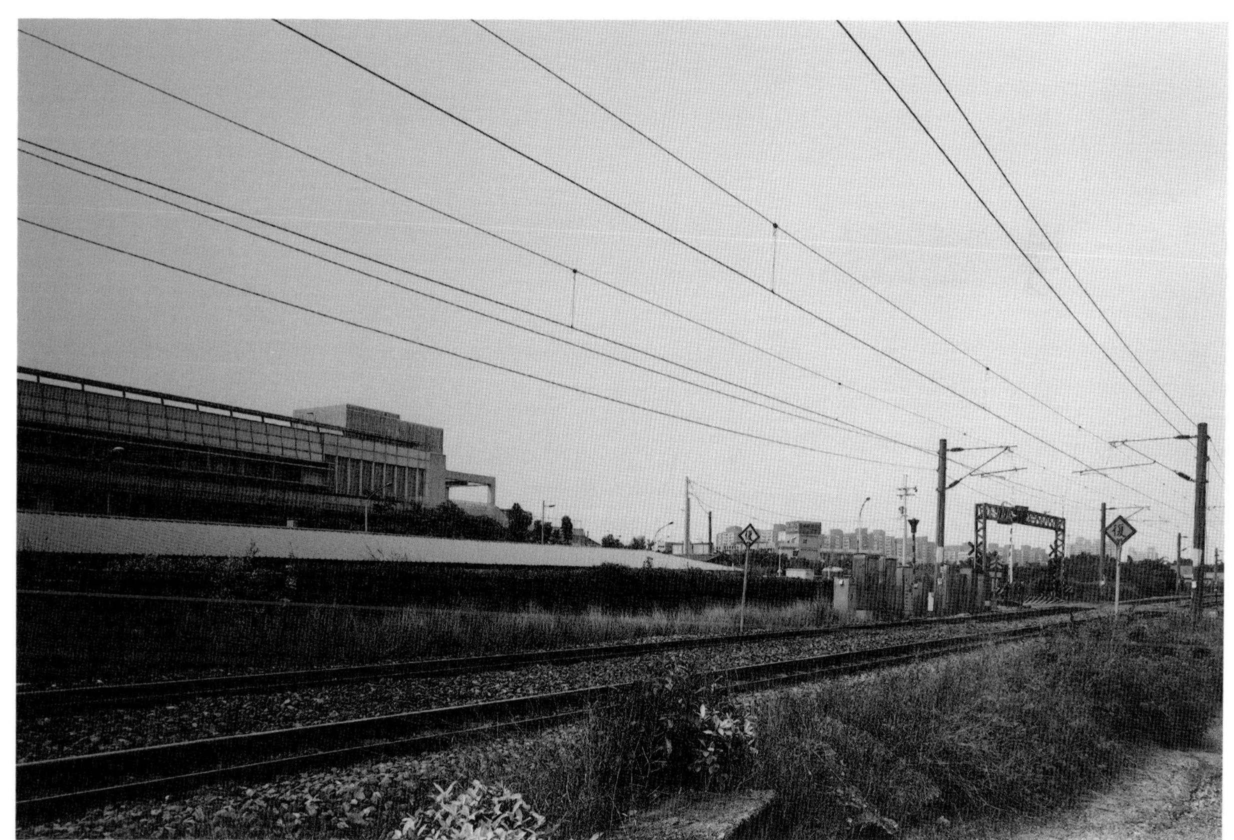

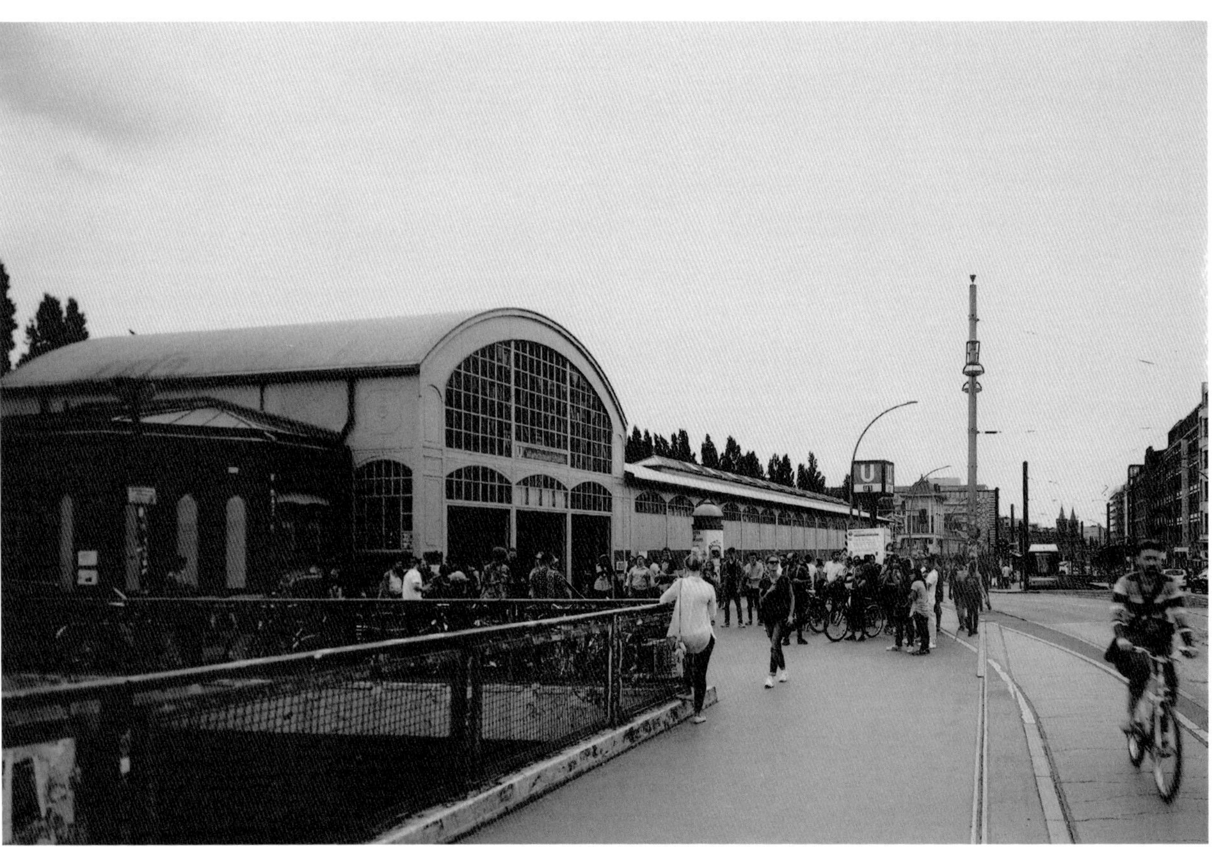

Warschauerstraße
Station, U1 Line

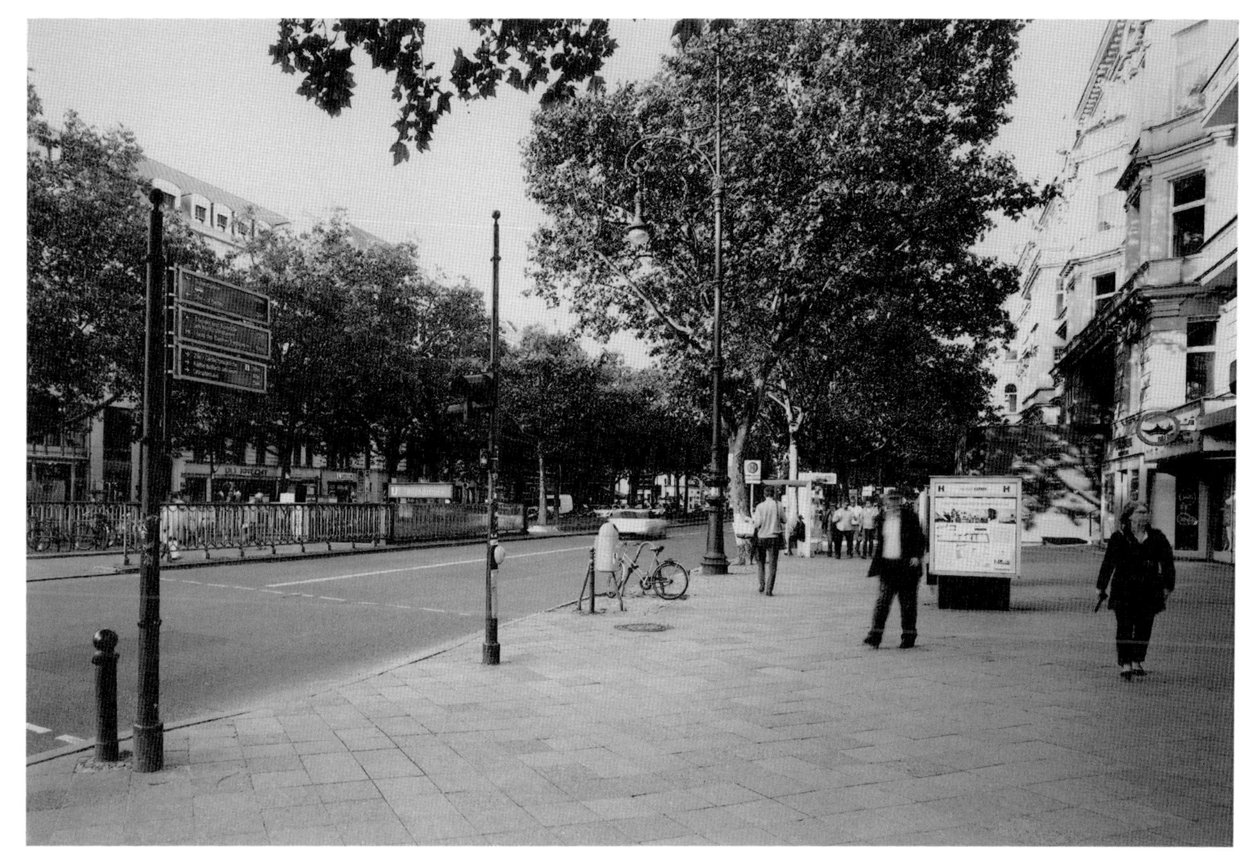

Berlin
< >
Uhlandstraße
Station, U1 Line

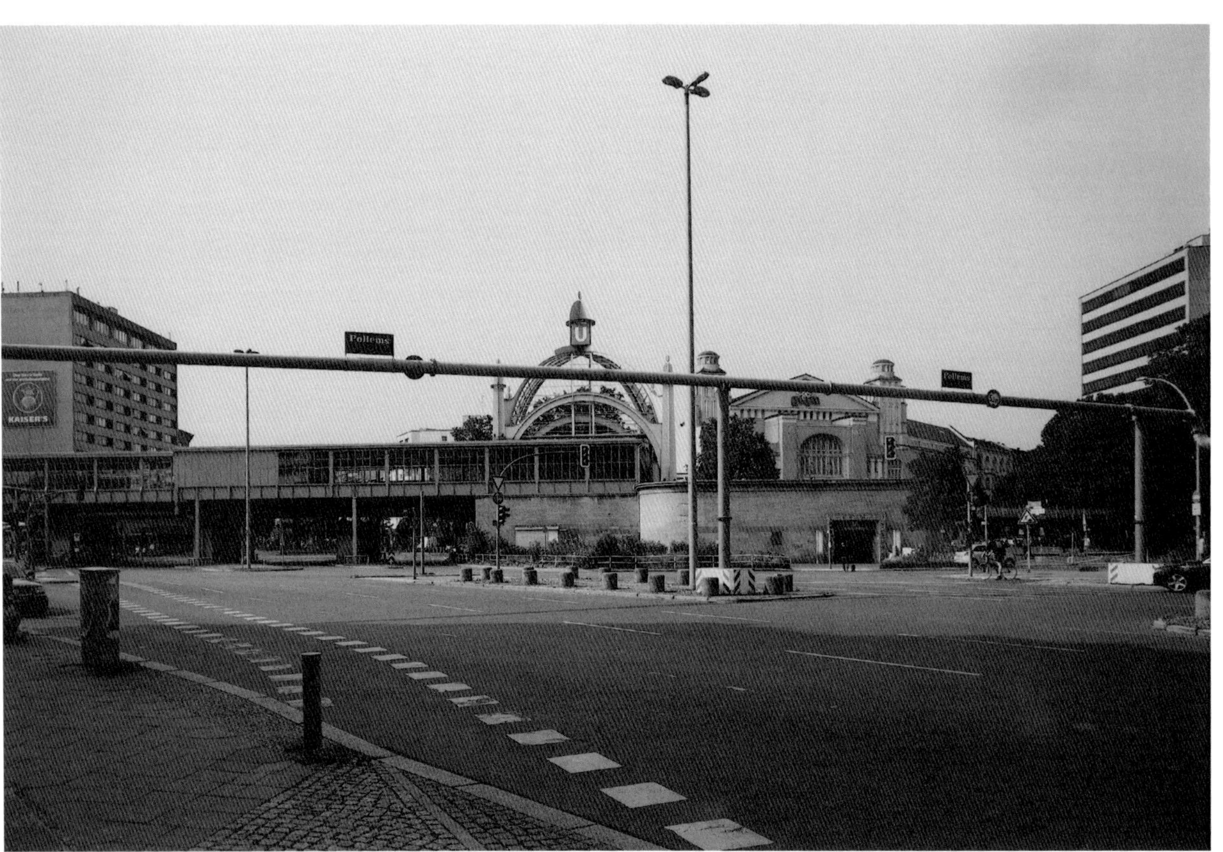

Nollendorf Platz
Station, U4 Line

Berlin
< >
Rathaus Spandau
Station, U7 Line

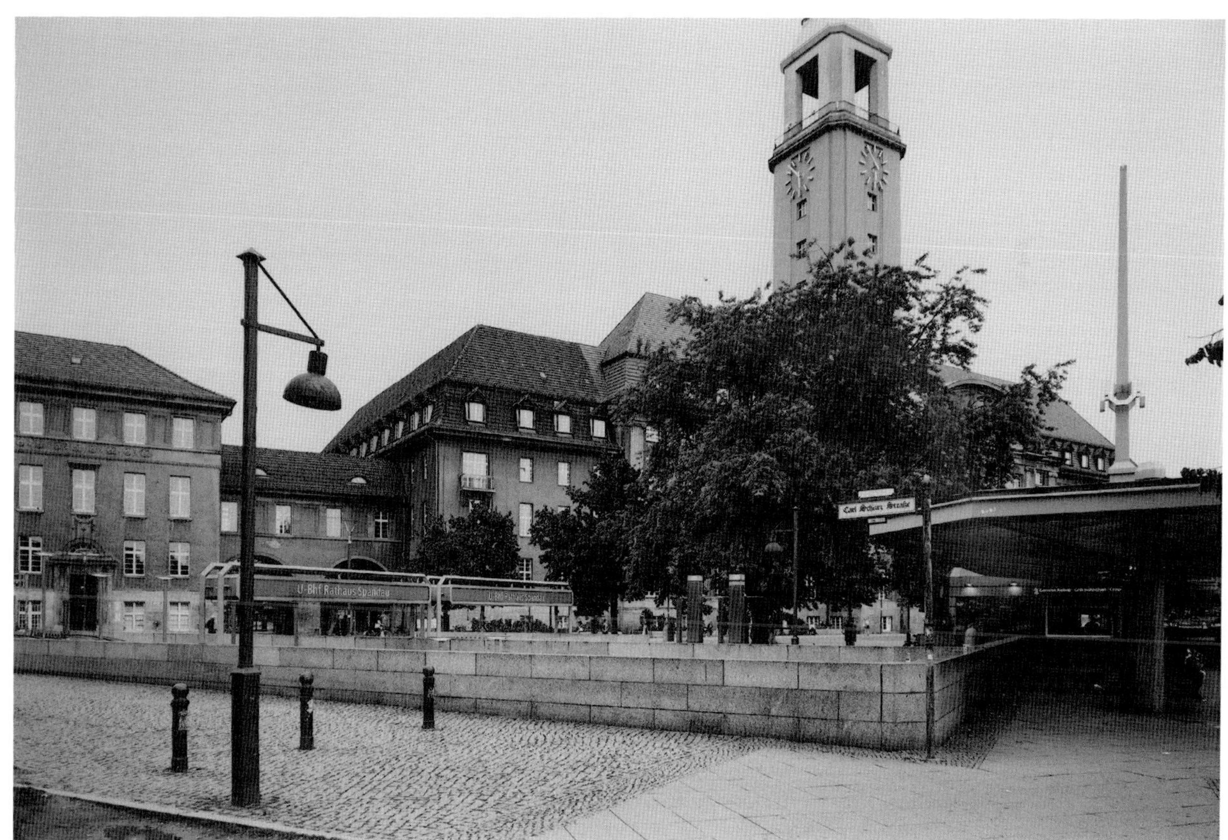

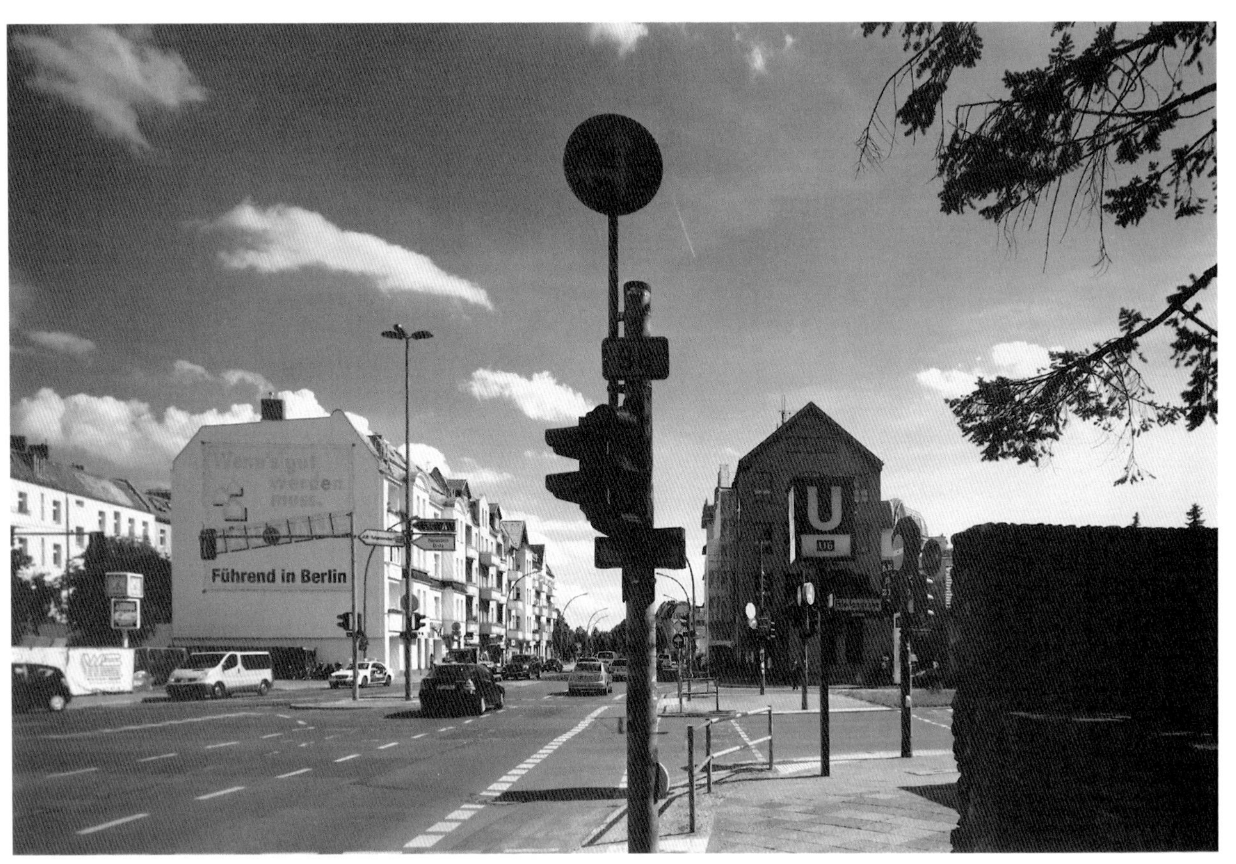

Alt Mariendorf
Station, U6 Line

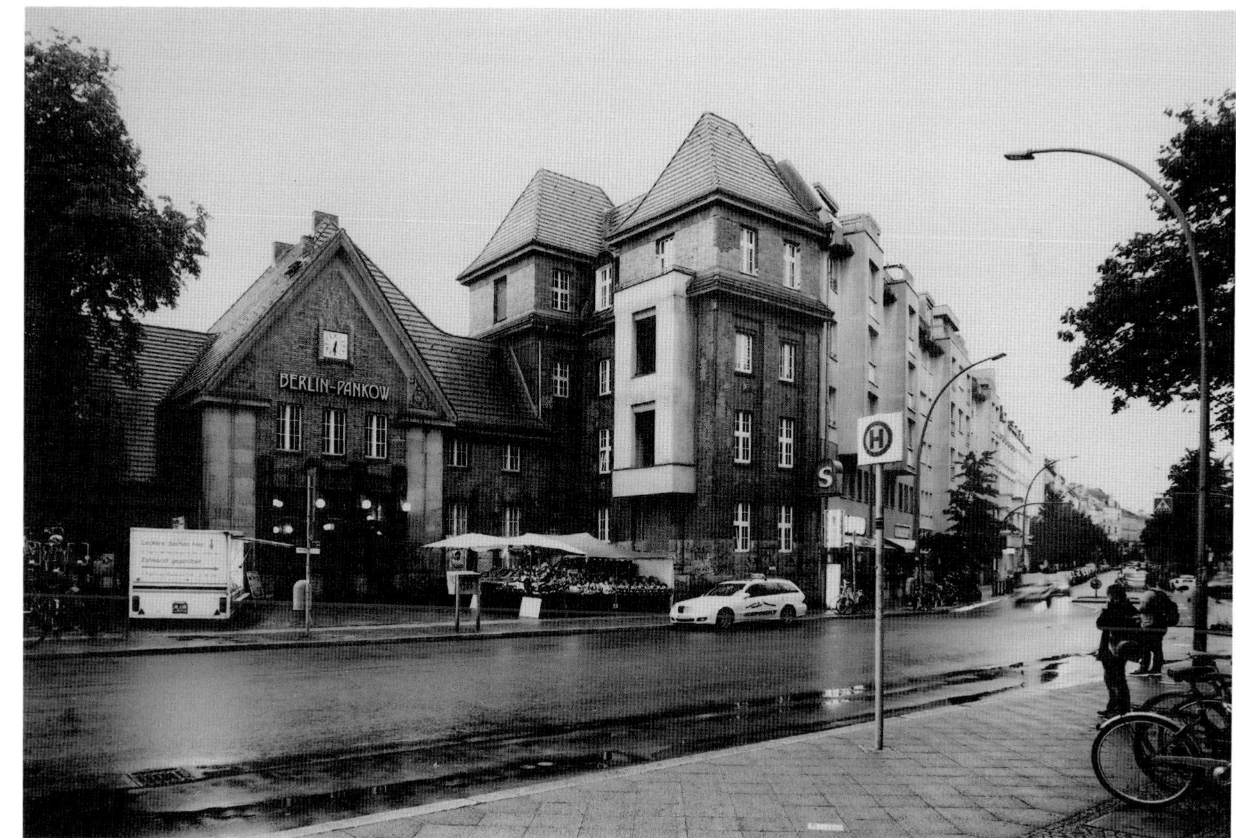

Berlin
< >
Pankow Station,
U2 Line

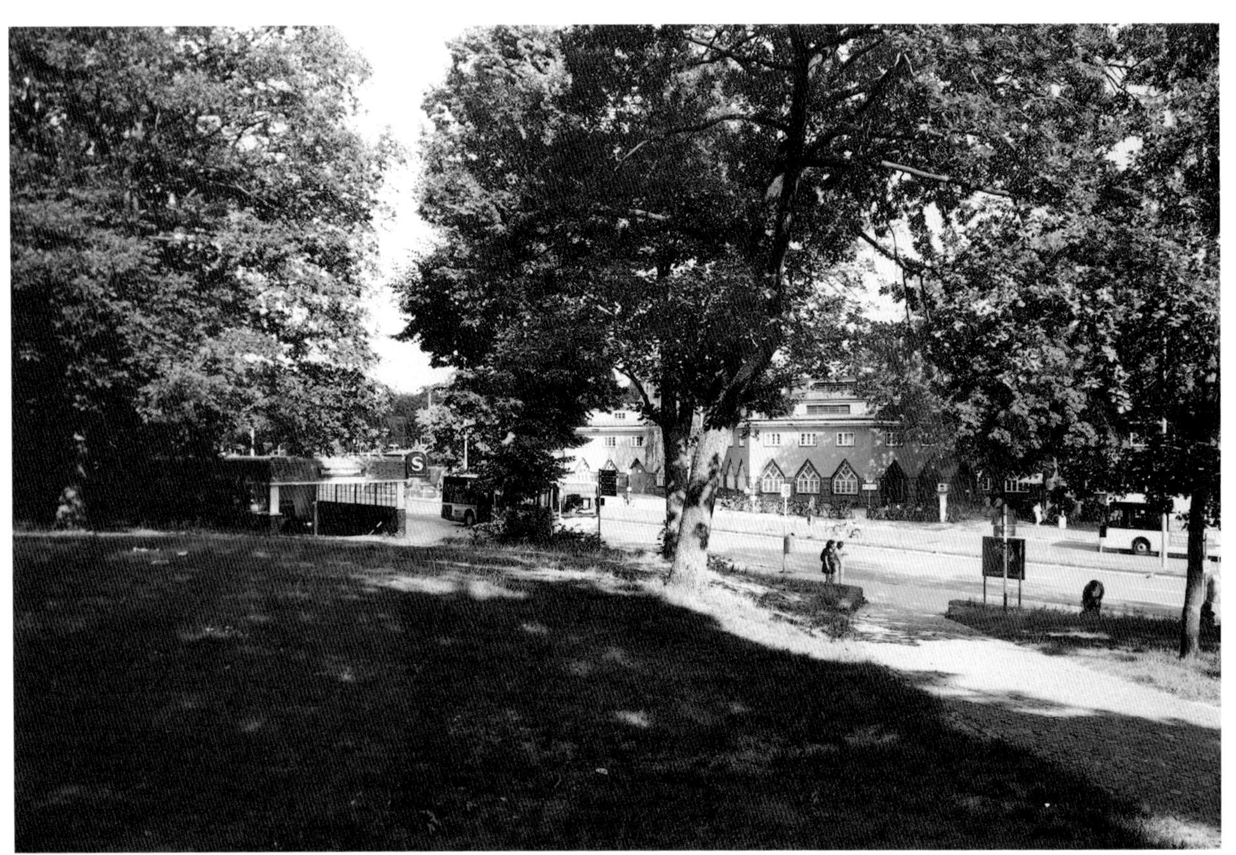

WanSee Station,
S1 Line

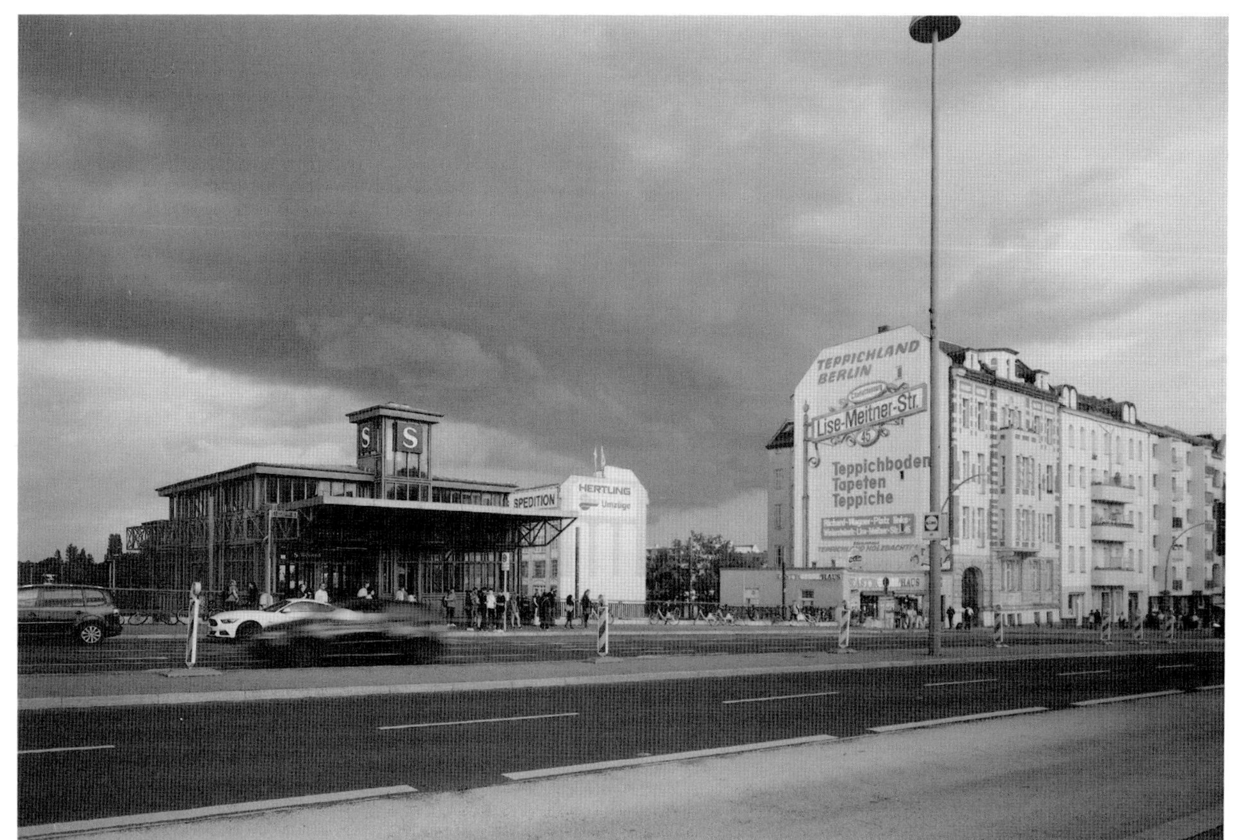

Berlin
< >
Westend Station,
S46 Line

note
the graphics apparatus of this book, including the maps of the four main cities of the investigation, was developed by Alessandro Martinelli and Yu-Chen Chiang in the context of the research activities at the Department of Landscape architecture, Chinese Culture University, Taipei.

Published by
LISt Lab
info@listlab.eu
listlab.eu

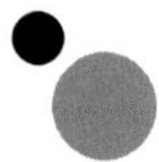

Editorial Director
Alessandro Franceschini

Author
Adriano Maccone,
Alessandro Martinelli

Editor
Alessandro Martinelli
as-ma.org

Art Director, Graphic Design & Produzione
Blacklist Creative, BCN
blacklist-creative.com

ISBN 9788898774517

Printed and bound in European Union,
July 2018

Promotion and distribution in Italy
Messaggerie Libri, Spa, Milano,
Numero verde 800.804.900
assistenza.ordini@meli.it;

International promotion and distribution
ACC Book Distribution Ltd
Woodbridge, Suffolk, IP12 4SD, UK
sales@antique-acc.com

LISt Lab is an editorial workshop, based in Europe, that works on contemporary issues. LISt Lab not only publishes, but also researches, proposes, promotes, produces, creates networks.

LISt Lab is a green company committed to respect the environment. Paper, ink, glues and all processings come from short supply chains and aim at limiting pollution. The print run of books and magazines is based on consumption patterns, thus preventing waste of paper and surpluses. LISt Lab aims at the responsibility of the authors and markets, towards the knowledge of a new publishing culture based on resource management.